Marianne R. M........t
18/9/07,

10

TARGET – ROMMEL!

TARGET – ROMMEL!

Robert Jackson

Weidenfeld and Nicolson
London

Copyright © 1991 by Robert Jackson
Published in Great Britain in 1991 by
George Weidenfeld and Nicolson Limited
91 Clapham High Street London SW4 7TA

British Library Cataloguing in Publication Data
is available

ISBN 0 297 84043 6

Typeset at The Spartan Press Ltd, Lymington, Hants
Printed in Great Britain by
Butler & Tanner Ltd, Frome and London

CHAPTER ONE

The chateau stood in a great loop of the river Seine, strong and formidable, its back towards a high cliff, its face towards the south and most of the day's sunlight. It had stood there for nine hundred years, ever since a man who was not yet styled the Conqueror had caused it to be built and had placed a trusted knight called Ronsceville in it, charging him with the defence of this part of the Duchy of Normandy. The chateau was flanked by tall cedars and meadows which, in the spring, were laden with cowslips.

The Ronscevilles had been there for nine hundred years, too, apart from a period when they had taken refuge in Spain to escape the guillotine. It had not been a long absence; they had returned twenty-five years later, in the wake of Napoleon's wars, to renewed sanity and a restored monarchy, and in the decades that followed they had lovingly brought back the chateau to its former glory.

The Ronscevilles who occupied the chateau in this early summer of 1944 were the duke, his duchess, their daughter and her two young sons. In bearing and appearance, they were much like the generations of Ronscevilles who had gone before them, but there was one major difference.

The present Ronscevilles had been reduced to the status of tenants.

The real landlord sat at an inlaid Renaissance desk in the great ducal hall. The room was draped with priceless tapestries and hung with oil paintings. It was imbued with the smell of musty books and centuries of wax polishing.

The man at the desk had been writing steadily for two hours, without interruption. Now, at last, he sat upright in his chair, carefully screwed the top back on his fountain pen, and laid it aside. He placed a hand behind him and massaged his back, wincing a little, because his lumbago – although not as bad as it had been during the winter months – still troubled him from time to time, especially when he sat at his desk.

He gathered together his papers, shuffled them until they lay neatly together, and placed them in a buff folder. Then he picked up a little bell that lay on the desk top and shook it. In the great hall, its clamour was surprisingly loud.

With scarcely any delay, the double doors at the far end of the hall opened and an aide came in. The newcomer was a captain; he wore the black uniform of the *Panzer* troops and was highly decorated. He marched across the room, halted smartly in front of the desk and clicked his heels. The seated man picked up the folder and handed it to him.

'Take that to Colonel Tempelhoff, Hellmuth. Tell him it's for distribution to all sector commanders. Immediate distribution. Needless to say, it's a list of their shortcomings, pursuant to my tour of inspection last week. And please ask Admiral Ruge to join me in the rose garden.'

'*Jawohl, Herr Feldmarschall.*' Captain Hellmuth Lang clicked his heels again and strode from the room, the buff folder under his arm.

The man at the desk watched his aide's retreating back until it disappeared behind the closed doors and then gave a sigh, massaging his temples with the thumb and forefinger of his right hand. If only all my subordinates were of the same calibre as Lang, he thought. Or the calibre of the operations officer, Tempelhoff, for that matter.

Field Marshal Erwin Rommel rose stiffly from the table, massaged his aching back again and straightened his tunic. Feeling better with every step, he crossed the hall and opened the door through which Lang had recently made his exit. Two helmeted sentries slammed to attention in the foyer and

Rommel nodded an acknowledgment to their salute as he strolled past, hands clasped behind his back.

Outside the chateau the air was fresh and warm. It had rained in the hours before dawn, and the flowers that packed the gardens surrounding the old building made the day heady with their scent. Conscious that other sentries who were stationed in the grounds had their watchful eyes upon him, Rommel crunched his way along a gravelled path and came to the rose garden, lowering himself into a wicker chair beside a small wrought-iron table. He placed his hands behind his neck and relaxed, gazing up at the few clouds that marched slowly across the sky, and let his thoughts wander idly.

It was the twenty-fourth of May, and everything was still quiet. As yet the Allies had not attempted their expected invasion, and Rommel was confident that they would not do so until at least the twentieth of June. He had personally checked the moon and tide tables, and there were no suitable invasion tides until then. So, there was time enough to snatch a few days with Lucie before the storm broke.

He missed Lucie, and the comfortable routine of their villa at Herrlingen, near Ulm; the fact that it had once been a Jewish old people's home, confiscated by the state in 1942, did not trouble him in the slightest. He missed waking up relaxed, with nothing to do in the morning but listen to the seven o'clock news, bathe and shave before making a leisurely breakfast on Lucie's excellent clear soup, and strolling to his heart's content in the gardens – or perhaps shooting in the nearby woods – until lunchtime.

Yet there was something he missed even more. He missed the scorching desert wind, and the star-festooned nights that chilled a man to the bone. He missed the sudden blossoming of the desert flowers, and their equally sudden passing. He missed the stench of diesel engines, the rattling tank tracks, the clouds of drifting dust. Above all, he missed the cameraderie of his beloved *Afrika Korps*.

All that was gone now, and he was glad that he had not been there to witness the end. He had come close, so very close, to victory during those hectic, wonderful days when his

Panzers had taken all before them and thundered across the desert towards Alexandria and, beyond that, the Nile Delta and the Suez Canal, the ultimate goal whose seizure would have chopped the British Empire in half and closed off the Mediterranean.

But a barren place called El Alamein, and a determined British general named Montgomery, had destroyed those dreams for good, and had hurled the *Panzers* back over the long desert road to their final defeat in Tunisia in the spring of 1943. Rommel, who by that time had been appointed to a staff job with the High Command, had been able to console himself only with one thought. Montgomery was not a better general; it was merely that the British had enjoyed more of everything, more tanks, more guns, more aircraft. And the final nail in the *Afrika Korps*' coffin had been driven home in November 1942, when the British and Americans had landed in Algeria.

Still, it was no use brooding over the loss of Africa now. The *Endkampf*, the last battle, had yet to be fought, and it would be fought here on the Atlantic coast. That, since last November, had been Rommel's new task: to ensure that the so-called Atlantic Wall was strong enough to throw the Allies back into the sea, once the invasion came.

He had done all he could, during the past six months, and had achieved much. A great deal of his energies had been devoted to reinforcing the defences of the Bay of the Seine; the heavy batteries of Cherbourg and Le Havre, supported by at least thirty others, overlapped the whole area, and could saturate the beaches and the sea approaches with their fire. Behind the great mass of obstacles and mines planted in the sea approaches and the beaches lay anti-tank defences, concrete strongpoints and earthworks backed by a formidable countryside ideally suited to defence.

Like an ugly rash, Rommel's beach obstacles had sprung up all along the coast of north-west Europe, from the Netherlands to Brittany. There were concrete and steel tetrahedra, concrete dragon's teeth, jagged steel 'hedgehogs' welded from girders at right angles, and many other devices, all designed to rip landing craft to pieces. Heavy timber stakes had been embedded into the beaches below the water mark; these and other obstacles had mines, iron spikes and jagged steel plates clamped to them. Millions more mines made the beaches a lethal killing zone for anyone who set foot on them.

There was more. Behind the beaches, in the sectors of France and Belgium opposite England, Rommel had created a Death Zone, a six-mile-deep swathe of land along the coast. As a last resort, he had the power to raze every building in this zone, to give his artillery a good field of fire, and to flood the land by damming rivers or letting in the sea.

And still, deep within him, he was tormented by the fear that all this might not be enough.

A man in naval uniform came striding into the garden, smiling broadly. He saluted Rommel – not with the Nazi salute, which both men disdained except on ceremonial occasions, when it was the order of the day – but with the salute of the old Imperial German Navy, the fingertips of the right hand stopping just short of the cap's peak, palm turned inwards.

Rommel smiled back and waved a hand. 'Sit down, Friedrich,' he invited. 'It was thoughtless of me. I should have ordered coffee.'

'I have taken the liberty of doing so, *Herr Feldmarschall*,' Vice-Admiral Friedrich Ruge informed him mildly. 'We may as well take advantage of this good French coffee, while it lasts.'

Rommel chuckled. Ruge was a Swabian, like himself, and had a cocky sense of humour which Rommel appreciated but did not share. His own humour was inclined to rudeness, and people who did not know him sometimes took it amiss. But underneath Ruge's humour there lay real talent; the man was a first-class coastal defence expert, which was why Rommel had brought him on to his staff.

Ruge sat down in a chair on the opposite side of the little table and looked expectantly at his superior, at the same time removing his cap. Rommel's face grew serious.

9

'Friedrich, there are certain aspects of our coastal defences which make me unhappy,' he said. 'I have just completed the report on my recent tour of inspection; a copy will be on your desk within hours, but I wanted to have a word with you first.'

He drummed his fingers on the table top. 'The dummy minefields, for example, which we have taken great pains to publicize for the enemy's benefit by placing warning notices all around them. There are cows grazing in them. Even the most stupid English intelligence officer, Friedrich, must be aware that cows are not permitted to graze in minefields. Then there are the gun positions, the batteries dug in to the rear of the beaches. Some of them are covered with black tarpaulins. I ask you, Friedrich, *black tarpaulins*! My God, are we presenting this information as a gift to the English reconnaissance pilots?'

He threw up his hands in despair and shook his head. 'There are other problems, too. Technical problems. The timber obstacles which we have driven into the sea bed everywhere, for example. Recently, one of our local sector commanders, on his own initiative, decided to test these defences with a 120-ton British landing craft, one of those we captured at Dieppe a couple of years ago. It went through the obstacles like a knife through butter. There were no mines attached to them, of course, but even so . . .'

He shook his head again. 'There has not been enough time, Friedrich. Not enough time to build up the defences to the level I would have wished, or to test them under realistic conditions. I have written a note to the sector commander, complimenting him, although in reality I could cheerfully wring his neck for presenting me with one more worry. But do you know what causes me the greatest anxiety?'

'The armour, *Herr Feldmarschall*,' Ruge stated in a matter-of-fact voice. He had already heard the argument several times.

'Correct, Friedrich,' Rommel agreed, 'the armour.' He suddenly slammed his clenched fist down on the table top, making Ruge start. 'We *must* bring our mechanised divisions into action in the first few hours,' he emphasised. 'Then I am

10

convinced that the enemy assault on our coast will be defeated on the very first day. But the *Panzer* divisions have still not been placed under my control, and they are still lying much too far back from the coast. The 12th ss *Panzer* division is dispersed all over the place, and the 2nd *Panzer* is more than fifty miles from the coast in the Somme sector. What would happen if the enemy were to drop strong paratroop forces, equipped for anti-tank operations, in the open space between the *Panzers* and the coast? It's a crazy situation, and that fellow Geyr isn't helping matters.'

Rommel was referring to General Geyr, who was an aristocrat – a baron – and looked down with some disdain on anyone who was not. He was in charge of the German tank forces in France, and he was opposed to Rommel's proposed tactics.

'I am an experienced tank commander,' Rommel snapped to his captive audience of one. 'We could fight mobile battles in the desert, but we can't do that here. You can't do it because the enemy's warships will bring their long-range guns to bear, and in any case they will have air superiority. And that's another point. That arsehole in the Berghof promised me a thousand aircraft; where are they?'

Ruge stirred uneasily in his chair and glanced around him. 'I wish you wouldn't say things like that, Erwin,' he said quietly, forgetting formality in his anxiety. 'It's dangerous. You don't know who might be listening, even here, and you could get yourself into the most terrible trouble.'

Rommel waved a hand airily. 'Oh, don't worry, Friedrich. I'm loyal enough. I'll do my duty, just as I have always done. But it annoys me when I'm asked to work miracles on a shoestring. It annoys me very much.'

At that moment an orderly appeared in the rose garden, bearing a silver tray with a coffee pot and cups on it. He placed the tray on the table, poured out the coffee, and departed with a small bow. Rommel waited until he was out of earshot, then grinned and said:

'Very elegant. You know, Friedrich, I'm sure some of these chaps have part-time jobs as waiters in French cafes. They've probably got positions all lined up for themselves, for when the war is over.'

He raised his cup and took a sip of coffee, nodding in appreciation. Setting the cup down again, he said thoughtfully: 'You know, Friedrich, we have got to win this coming battle, here in the west. The whole outcome of the war, and the fate of the Reich, depends on it. Once we have forced a decision in our favour here, we can transfer the forty-five divisions we hold in Europe to the eastern front and stop the Russians in their tracks.'

Ruge raised an eyebrow. Privately, he did not share Rommel's optimism. Germany's war economy was already on the rocks. She lacked the raw materials that were necessary to build armaments, and she was running out of fuel. The dream of seizing Russia's Caucasus oilfields had died with the Sixth Army at Stalingrad, and any hope of regaining the initiative by means of a great armoured victory had been dashed at Kursk six months later. Ruge doubted whether even an extra forty-five divisions could stem the Russian tide.

Rommel had not seen, or had chosen to ignore, the scepticism on Ruge's face. 'The enemy's entire invasion operation must not be allowed to survive more than a few hours,' he went on. 'Take their landing at Dieppe, for example. Once defeated, I do not think that they would ever again try to invade. Quite apart from their enormous losses, and the fact that it would take months – perhaps years – to organise another attempt, an invasion failure would deal a crushing blow to British and American morale. Their leaders, Churchill and Roosevelt and the rest, would be dismissed as incompetents. That's what the *Führer* believes, too.'

Ruge also took a drink of coffee, then said: 'The main problem, in my view, is still not so much that we don't know when the invasion will take place, as *where*. Our intelligence on that score is virtually nil. We know about the enemy troop concentrations in southern England, for example, but their positioning could be part of an enormous bluff.'

Rommel nodded. 'As it undoubtedly is, Friedrich. Their

concentrations opposite the Pas de Calais are a little too obvious, and that is precisely what they want us to think. They want us to believe that they will land in Normandy, whereas they intend to push their invasion forces straight across the Channel, by the shortest possible route. You'll see.'

Ruge agreed with his superior, although his view was not shared by Admiral Krancke, the c-in-c Navy Group West. From the pattern of the enemy's bombing and minelaying efforts, and from the limited Luftwaffe air reconnaissance of southern England, Krancke had deduced that the enemy's main objectives were to be the ports of Le Havre and Cherbourg, and that meant a landing in Normandy.

What Rommel did not know was that for several months there had been a bitter personal feud between Krancke and Ruge, and that most of the Naval c-in-c's reports on the matter had never reached Rommel's headquarters.

It was as well that Rommel did not know it, for Ruge was one of the few men he trusted implicitly. As time went by, he was becoming more convinced that he, Rommel, was the only leader with sufficient experience and leadership to conduct the forthcoming battle on the beaches of western Europe, and in so doing save Germany from shameful defeat.

On the other side of the Channel, there were others who shared that opinion.

CHAPTER TWO

In its present form, St Paul's School in Hammersmith was eight hundred years younger than the chateau on the Seine, although as an institution it was venerable. The original building had been founded in 1509 by John Colet, Dean of St Paul's Cathedral, and at that time it had been the largest school in England, providing free education for 153 children. That first building, like the cathedral, had been destroyed in the Great Fire; the present structure at Hammersmith was the fourth in succession.

There were no pupils here now, the whole school having been evacuated to Crowthorne in Berkshire at the beginning of the war. Yet there was plenty of activity in the Hammersmith building, for it was here, in May 1944, that the destiny of Europe was being mapped out. These panelled walls now housed the headquarters of 21st Army Group, the military formation that would soon hurl the greatest armada in the history of warfare across the English Channel.

One of the principle architects of the forthcoming operation, the commander of the Allied land forces, sat at the desk in what had once been the headmaster's study. It was an environment that was familiar to him, for he had once been a pupil at St Paul's and had on occasions stood before this same desk, mainly to receive reprimands rather than accolades, for he had not been the brightest or most diligent of boys. Yet even then he had harboured dreams of where his own destiny might lead him, and the dream was about to be fulfilled. LAW

For General Sir Bernard Montgomery, Operation Overlord was more than an invasion, more than an avalanche of men and material. It was a crusade, and more than a quarter of a million men who were to storm the enemy-held coast would bear the red cross of St George upon their shoulders.

Montgomery paused briefly in his task of studying the latest intelligence reports on the German defences along the Normandy coastline – reports compiled through the efforts of gallant young men who slipped across the Channel under cover of darkness and who swam among the mined obstacles at terrible risk to gather their information – and glanced at the clock on the wall. It was seven forty-five, and he had been at his desk since six, following his morning work-out in the school's gymnasium.

The clock did not hold his attention for more than a moment, but the photograph that hung beside it did. He had put it there himself, to serve as a constant reminder of his greatest anxiety. It had travelled across the Western Desert with him, to be studied over and over again as he strove to pry into the mind of the man it portrayed and analyze his intentions.

The face of Erwin Rommel, the enemy commander most respected – and feared, if the truth were known – by Montgomery remained as inscrutable as ever. He sighed and returned to his paperwork.

Fifteen minutes later, Montgomery looked up again as someone rapped on the study door. It opened on his summons and his adjutant stepped into the room.

'Major Douglas, sir,' he announced.

Montgomery leaned back in his chair. 'Very good. Tell him to come in.'

The adjutant disappeared, leaving the door open. A moment later a man stood framed in it; a tall man, in battledress uniform and wearing a red beret. He stepped forward two paces and brought his right hand up in a crisp salute.

Montgomery nodded at him and pointed to a chair on the other side of the desk.

'Good morning, Douglas. Sit down,' he ordered, glancing again at the clock as he did so. It was precisely eight o'clock.

Major Callum Douglas had made a point of being exactly on time. Montgomery, a stickler for punctuality, did not like people to be late for appointments; neither did he like them to be early.

Douglas sat down and removed his beret. Montgomery looked hard at him and gave a thin smile, his nearest concession to a friendly gesture.

'I gather you chaps aren't too happy with your change of headgear,' he said.

Douglas looked at him in surprise, wondering if there was anything Montgomery didn't know.

'Well, sir, we'd got rather used to the old one,' he said. It was a very sore point with the men of the Special Air Service that they had recently been made to exchange their distinctive and much-coveted sand-coloured berets for the red ones worn by normal airborne troops, although they had been allowed to retain the SAS badge – a winged sword, King Arthur's Excalibur – and the motto, *Who Dares Wins*.

Montgomery grunted, and did not pursue the subject of berets any further. Instead, he asked:

'Have you settled in all right?'

Douglas, wondering a little at Montgomery's concern for his welfare, said that he had. He had arrived in London the previous evening, after a long and tiring journey from Ayr, where the SAS had a big training camp, and had been billeted in a very comfortable flat in Latymer Court, just across the road from St Paul's School. Most of the officers connected with HQ 21st Army Group were also lodged there, and security was very thorough. Breakfast had been something of a revelation to Douglas; as a newly promoted major he had been the most junior officer in the dining room. Everybody else, or so it seemed, was at least a brigadier. Or maybe it was just that all the other majors and lower forms of officer life got up early to avoid the crush.

Douglas had met Montgomery face to face only once before, in the spring of 1943, after Douglas's SAS detachment had carried out a successful operation to destroy a German headquarters in Tunisia. Montgomery now mentioned that meeting, and to his astonishment Douglas discovered that the general recalled every minute detail. He also knew everything about Douglas's subsequent career.

'I see that you and your men have been giving the enemy a difficult time,' Montgomery said. 'Your last operation was quite masterly; congratulations upon it.'

Earlier in the year, Douglas and his small SAS team, with the help of Polish resistance fighters, had carried out a devastating attack on a top-secret German rocket site on the Baltic coast. They had been picked up by a Russian flying boat and had only recently returned home after a long and arduous journey via the Middle East and the Mediterranean.

The army, with its customary generosity, had given them a fortnight's leave before sending them as instructors to Ayr. Douglas had taken advantage of the fortnight to roam the hills around the family home near Perth and let the clean Scottish wind blow the taste of killing out of his system. It was a rebirth he had undergone several times, since he had first gone to war.

His homecoming had been attended by sadness, for Colette had not been there. His French-born fiancée, so his father had explained apologetically, had been summoned for duty by the Special Operations Executive, the undercover organization that was responsible for the network of agents and saboteurs in occupied Europe. Colette had returned to England with Douglas after an operation involving the SAS and the French Resistance in southern France, an operation that had cost her father his life.

Ever since then she had lived with Douglas's own father, who had virtually adopted her as a daughter. James Douglas still chuckled over the fact that it was Colette who had proposed to his rather reticent son, instead of the other way round. He was glad, though, that they had decided to wait until the war was over before they married.

Colette had received word from the War Office that Douglas was safe, and several long letters had been awaiting him when he arrived home. They spoke of little, personal things that had been shared between them, and no more; they had given no indication of her whereabouts, but that was to be expected.

What worried him was the fact that there had been no telephone call. He did not care to dwell on the possible implications of that.

'How did you find our Russian allies?' Montgomery asked suddenly.

'A bit odd, sir,' Douglas admitted. 'Either very sullen or overbearingly friendly. I've compiled a report, setting out my impressions. I'm afraid they weren't terribly favourable.'

Montgomery nodded. 'I know, I've seen the report, Douglas. It's most interesting. We need to get inside the minds of those chaps, you know. We might have to fight them, one day,' he added, as though musing out loud.

'Still, never mind that. I expect you're wondering why I have brought you here.'

Montgomery stared at Douglas, the furrows around his eyes becoming deeper. Douglas was aware that there were furrows around his own eyes, too; the desert did that to a man.

The general waved a hand in the direction of the photograph on the wall.

'This fellow Rommel has cropped up again,' he said in his precise, clipped tones. 'He has been in charge of the coastal defences in the west for some months now, and believe me, he has given them a considerable shaking up. According to some reports, he is more in charge of things in general than is his supposed commander-in-chief, Field Marshal von Rundstedt. His direct access to Hitler for what he needs, and all that sort of thing.'

Montgomery cleared his throat and reached for a tumbler of water that stood on the desk top. The tumbler was covered with a neatly-folded napkin, which Montgomery removed and laid to one side while he took a few sips. He set the tumbler down, replaced the napkin and leaned forward, folding his hands on the desk.

'I wanted to see you personally, Douglas, because I require you to undertake a task of enormous importance. I know that you more than deserve a rest, but you are without doubt the best qualified man for the job I have in mind. No one has more experience of leading a professional fighting unit inside enemy territory than you.'

Douglas felt the now familiar churning in his stomach. Suddenly, it was all he could do to hold his breakfast down. He gripped the arms of his chair so that Montgomery would not notice that his hands were shaking. The feeling would pass – it always did pass – but while it lasted it was horrible and breath-stopping. He gazed at Montgomery without expression.

'I want you to go to France and kill Rommel,' Montgomery said. He might have been asking the SAS officer to join him for tea and biscuits. 'Of course, I'm asking you to volunteer.'

'Yes, sir.' There did not seem to be much else to say.

'Good man!' Montgomery smiled his thin smile again. 'Now, how long will it take you to get your team together?'

Douglas thought for a moment, then said: 'Not long, sir. A day or so. Most of them are at Ayr, instructing.'

'Good. Round them up. I will have a signal sent to Ayr, authorizing the release of your men from duty there. Speed is important; we have very little time.'

Montgomery paused for a moment, and regarded Douglas steadily before continuing.

'I am quite convinced that you are capable of carrying out this most difficult mission successfully. However, there is one thing I must tell you. It is not simply a matter of infiltrating into Rommel's headquarters and killing him; I want you to do the job at a precise time – and even I, at this moment, do not know when that will be.'

Douglas looked at him questioningly, inviting a further explanation. Montgomery provided it.

'You already know that the invasion of occupied Europe is very close, Douglas. In fact, the target date for all preparations to be complete is the first of June, four days from now. The invasion itself – D-Day – will take place at the earliest possible moment thereafter. There are certain favourable dates, which I do not propose to disclose, but a great deal depends on the prevailing weather conditions.

'The great thing is to catch the Germans on the hop,' Montgomery continued. 'To this end, the seaborne assault will be preceded by airborne landings, designed to secure key objectives in the rear areas and to hold up enemy reinforcements until the seaborne forces effect a breakout from the beach-heads. The French Resistance will also have a leading part to play. This aspect is of particular concern to you, because the plan is to put you in contact with a Resistance cell, which will give you all the assistance you need. You have worked with the Resistance before, I understand.'

'Yes, sir. We carried out an operation against an enemy airfield in southern France.'

Montgomery nodded. 'So you did. You will therefore be aware that the Special Operations Executive is in constant touch with the various Resistance cells scattered throughout France, and that instructions in the form of coded messages are passed to them by the BBC at regular intervals. One particular coded message will be the signal that the invasion is imminent, and that will be the moment for you to make your move. If we can remove Rommel from the scene at the very moment the invasion begins – and, with luck, dispose of some of his key staff officers as well – it will throw the German military command in the west into confusion for several vital hours. Rommel is a brilliant tactician, with a truly amazing flair for analyzing a situation and making the right moves. No other German commander comes anywhere near him in this respect.'

There was a lengthy silence in the headmaster's study as Douglas digested the information that had just been given to him. It was finally broken by Montgomery.

'Well, Douglas? D'you think you can do it?'

'We'll do our best, sir,' Douglas told him quietly. 'But I'll need all the information I can get on Rommel's routine, as well as on the layout of his HQ and so on.'

'That's all arranged.' Montgomery pressed a buzzer. A few moments later, a small man who looked as though he had slept in his uniform entered the room. His back was slightly hunched and he seemed unable to stand up straight. He put up an incredibly sloppy salute and peered at Montgomery through thick-lensed spectacles. Like Douglas, he wore a major's crowns; green shoulder flashes denoted that he belonged to the Intelligence Corps.

Douglas, knowing Montgomery's reputation for smartness and discipline, expected the general to throw a fit at the newcomer's untidy appearance. Instead, Montgomery nodded affably.

'Fitzroy, this is Douglas,' he said. Douglas rose and the two men shook hands. Behind the thick lenses, Fitzroy's eyes twinkled with humour. Douglas took an instinctive liking to him. If Montgomery felt able to tolerate his appearance, he must be somebody quite special.

'Fitzroy, you know why Douglas is here,' Montgomery said. 'Take him away and brief him thoroughly. Good luck to you, Douglas.'

'Thank you, sir.' Douglas replaced his beret and saluted the lonely man behind the desk, a man on whose expertise and thoroughness the fate of millions rested; a man who soldiers in earlier campaigns had nicknamed, perhaps unjustly, the gravedigger. Montgomery, absorbed once more in his daily reports, did not look up.

Fitzroy led the SAS officer down a series of corridors, all of them with armed sentries stationed at every turn. The two men ascended a spiral staircase and reached what appeared to have been the dormitory floor. Fitzroy halted at a door on the left of the landing and, producing an enormous bunch of keys from his tunic pocket, unlocked it. He reached round the door jamb to switch on an electric light, then ushered Douglas inside. As soon as they were both in, Fitzroy locked the door behind them.

Douglas looked around. They were in a medium-sized, windowless room which, Douglas decided, had probably once been used to store bedding or luggage, or perhaps both.

The walls were plastered with photographs, mostly cut from newspapers and magazines, and all depicting one subject: Erwin Rommel. The field marshal gazed down on Douglas from the turret of a tank in the Battle of France, looked up at him from an improvised chart table in the desert, peered at him from astride the carcase of a wild boar in some German forest.

But what captured Douglas's attention was the splendid model that stood on a table in the centre of the room, taking up most of the available space. Fitzroy crabbed his way around it, beaming like a small boy about to show off a new model railway.

'What do you think of it, old boy? All my own work, you know. I've been building it since January, in my spare time. Do take a closer look.'

Douglas did. He inspected the model in fine detail, from the anti-aircraft guns that ringed it to the half-ruined Norman tower that surmounted it, perched high on the cliff above.

'It's absolutely splendid,' he said, and Fitzroy's face glowed at the compliment. 'Rommel's country residence, I presume?'

'As a matter of fact, it's the permanent command post of Army Group B,' the intelligence officer told him. 'Look, do you see these tunnels here?'

He pointed to some small circular holes which he had faithfully reproduced in his papier mâché cliff. Douglas nodded. 'Well,' Fitzroy continued, 'those lead to extra quarters which the Germans blasted out to accommodate Rommel's Army Group staff. They sleep underground, snug as bugs in rugs, so our nasty air raids don't disturb them. Rommel doesn't sleep there, though; his quarters are here.'

He pointed to miniature French windows which he had created in one side of the model chateau. 'The room leads directly into the grounds, as you can see,' Fitzroy explained. 'Rommel likes to potter around the flower beds first thing in the morning, apparently.'

'Well, I'll be damned! How do you know all this?'

Fitzroy tapped the side of his nose, eyes twinkling. 'Spies everywhere, old chap. Spies everywhere. Oddly enough, the area isn't saturated with bodyguards and the like, as you might imagine; Rommel apparently gets on pretty well with the local French people. Legendary figure and all that, you know. They seem pretty relieved that he's running the show, instead of some absolute swine. Anyway, it all works out to our advantage. There's a steady flow of information reaching us all the time on what Rommel is up to.'

Douglas peered at the model again. 'Hm. Just one thing – where is it?'

Fitzroy apologized. 'Sorry, old chap, should have told you that straightaway. It's half-way down the Seine, where the river loops northwards between Mantes and Vernon. Lovely bit of countryside . . . I used to spend quite a few holidays there, before the war,' he added nostalgically.

Douglas looked at him. 'That's interesting. So you know the countryside pretty well?'

'Tolerably so,' Fitzroy said. 'But wait a moment – I've got a map somewhere. You can see for yourself what the terrain is like. It's about sixty miles from the coast, by the way.'

He bent down and pulled a cardboard box from under the table, rummaging in it until he found the map. He handed it to Douglas, who studied it in silence for a few minutes. Eventually, he commented: 'I can see why the castle was picked as an HQ. It must be pretty well immune to air attack, with this cliff in the way. Not to mention these anti-aircraft batteries.' He pointed at the model. 'Are they represented accurately?'

Fitzroy looked offended. 'But of course, old boy. I update them every week. In any case, only the ones in the grounds are mobile. Those on the cliff top are well dug in. They're there for the duration.'

Douglas grinned disarmingly. 'All right, I'm sorry. I didn't mean to cast doubts on your handiwork. Look, my name's Callum – what's yours?'

'Walter,' the intelligence officer told him solemnly. 'Bloody awful name, but I'm told it goes with Fitzroy. Sounds aristocratic – which, incidentally, I am not.'

He took the map from Douglas and replaced it in the cardboard box. 'I say, it gets a bit claustrophobic in here, and

I daren't leave the door ajar in case somebody peeps in who shouldn't. Why don't we take a stroll up the road to Holland Park, and carry on the conversation in a more civilized manner? It's a lovely morning, and I could do with some fresh air. To tell the truth, I've got a bit of a hangover,' he added ruefully.

A few minutes later, Fitzroy having first called in at his office to tell his staff that he would be absent for a while, the two men were walking eastwards along Hammersmith Road, anonymous figures in the crowds of people heading for their shops and offices as wartime London began its working day. As they walked, they learned something of each other's military career. Douglas found out that Fitzroy was fluent in several languages, including French and German.

'I worked in a bank in Paris before the war,' he said, 'and then in 1939 I was transferred to the Berlin branch. Got out by the skin of my teeth, on one of the last trains to cross the border before war was declared. The train was bound for Paris, and as I was flat broke I called at our embassy there to try and scrounge a few bob for my fare home. Instead, I found myself bundled into uniform, made an instant lance-corporal and attached to the Field Security Police, which was the forerunner of the Intelligence Corps. Spent weeks rushing round Belgium looking for fifth columnists disguised as nuns, and that sort of thing. Never found any, of course; the whole tale was absolute rubbish.'

Fitzroy laughed suddenly. 'You wouldn't believe the rumours that were flying around, especially after the Germans attacked. Any priest or nun wandering around on their own was liable to be locked up. Anyway, I eventually did get home, on a boat from Dunkirk. Were you with the Expeditionary Force?'

Douglas shook his head. 'No, I was still training then. Went out to Egypt with the 20th Hussars at the beginning of '41. We had it pretty well all our own way, until Rommel showed up. It was hard after that.'

Memories. Flimsy little Stuart light tanks scurrying, shattering and burning amid the smoke and swirling sand as the

Panzer IIIs and the deadly eighty-eight millimetre guns picked them off. Men trapped and screaming in flames. *Stuka* dive-bombers, screeching down to pound the British armour as it streamed back in disorder over the Egyptian frontier. The brilliant leadership of General Sir Claude Auchinleck, Commander-in-Chief of the Middle East Land Forces, taking personal command of the battered Eighth Army just in time to save it from crushing defeat.

'I'll bet,' Fitzroy said, interrupting his thoughts. 'So was Dieppe.'

Douglas looked at him in surprise. 'You were at Dieppe?'

'Not by choice, old boy. I was commissioned by this time – it's amazing what an idle life on the staff can do for a chap's chances of promotion – and they sent me over to Dieppe at the head of a small team of German speakers to interrogate prisoners. It didn't quite work out like that, because as you know it was the Germans who took most of the prisoners.'

The raid on Dieppe, carried out in August 1942, had ended in disaster. The troops taking part – mainly men of the 2nd Canadian Division, supported by British commandos and a detachment of US Rangers – had suffered appalling losses. The enemy had been ready and waiting, and nearly one-half of the attacking force had stayed in France, dead or prisoners of war.

Fitzroy did not elaborate on his Dieppe experiences, and Douglas sensed that he had no wish to talk about them.

'They sent me to Sicily in 1943,' the intelligence officer continued, 'and then I spent some time in Italy with No. 1 Special Force. I quite enjoyed it there; I enjoy pottering around ancient ruins, you know. Unfortunately, I was whisked back here when Monty was given his present job.'

They passed Olympia, entered Kensington High Street and turned left into Holland Walk, which ran along the eastern side of the park. The iron railings had long since gone, to be melted down and turned into tanks.

The park itself was quiet, apart from the chattering of the sparrows which darted among the branches of the trees and flitted around the brickwork of the ruined house. An imposing Jacobean building, Holland House had been on the receiving end of a stick of German bombs in 1940 and had lain derelict ever since, sealed off from the rest of the park by coils of barbed wire, presumably for the safety of the public. Slit trenches, to serve as makeshift air-raid shelters, had been dug at various points around the park, and at one point a clump of trees had been felled to provide a clear field of fire for an anti-aircraft battery. The battery had since been removed.

Apart from a couple of elderly ladies seated on a bench reading their morning newspapers, the park was deserted. There was no fear that what passed between Fitzroy and Douglas might be overheard.

For the next hour, as they strolled along the pathways between the trees, Fitzroy talked about Rommel; his habits, his routines, the structure of his military command in France. Douglas was astonished at the man's depth of knowledge. By the time Fitzroy had finished, he felt that he had become intimately acquainted with the enemy field marshal.

At length, Fitzroy stopped in his tracks and looked up at the taller man.

'Well, that's about it,' he said. 'I've told you pretty well all I can about your target. I suggest you now spend the rest of the day memorizing every detail of his headquarters.' He smiled. 'You can actually lift the roof off the model and look inside.'

He glanced up at the sky. 'It's turning cloudy,' he said. 'Shouldn't be at all surprised if we get some rain. We'd better be getting back.'

As they walked towards the edge of the park, Fitzroy paused again and looked at the ruined house. 'What a sad thing,' he said. 'That lovely old building. I wonder if it will ever be restored.'

'I suppose there's one consolation,' Douglas commented. 'London withstood the worst Hitler could throw at her, and survived. Those bad times are over now, don't you think?'

Fitzroy made no reply. His thoughts were busy with a dark secret about which Douglas knew nothing. Nor, mercifully, did the people of London, who might soon have to face a new and even more sinister ordeal.

On the other side of the Channel, the Germans had been building dozens of concrete ramps. British Intelligence knew their purpose: they were designed to launch a new, jet-propelled pilotless flying bomb, its nose packed with a ton of high explosive. The bomb was already being mass-produced; according to the latest estimates, it would be operational within weeks. And all the ramps were pointing towards London.

There were rumours that the Germans were developing other secret weapons, too, weapons so devastating that they had the power to destroy an entire city.

That, above all, was why the coming invasion had to succeed.

CHAPTER THREE

Low clouds swept across the airfield, driven before a strong south-westerly wind. Squalls of rain fell from them, spattering on the blacked-out windows of the stone cottage that stood close to the field's perimeter. The rain fell, too, on the camouflaged wings of the Spitfires that were dispersed in sandbagged revetments around the field, and on the Lockheed Hudson bomber that stood apart from the other aircraft, not far from the stone cottage.

The twin-engined Hudson contrasted sharply with the Spitfires, not only because it lacked their rakish lines, but because it was painted matt black all over. It bore no RAF roundels or identification markings of any kind.

The young men who flew the Spitfires from RAF station Tangmere, nestling on the edge of the South Downs near the Sussex town of Chichester, were used to the comings and goings of strange, black-painted aircraft. Sometimes they were Hudsons; more often they were high-winged Lysanders.

The Spitfire pilots never saw the men who flew the black-painted machines, and had no idea who, or what, they carried when they disappeared into the night, heading out over the Channel. Also, they knew better than to ask questions. They knew only that the mysterious aircraft came and went during the moon period.

In fact, the crew of the Hudson that stood in black silence on the airfield sat in the kitchen of the stone cottage. There were only two men – pilot and navigator – and the laden ashtray that stood on the table between them was indicative of their nervous tension, although neither showed signs of it in his expression. Only the pilot, who was leafing through a copy of *Punch*, allowed his eyes to stray towards the telephone by his elbow from time to time, as though willing it to ring.

When it did ring, pilot and navigator made a simultaneous grab for it. The pilot got there first. He raised the receiver to his ear and listened intently for a few moments, then said:

'Okay, thanks. Get the ground crew across, would you?'

He replaced the receiver and looked at the navigator. 'It's on, George,' he said, his accent betraying Australian origins. He pointed a finger at the ceiling, and the weather beyond it. 'This lot's going to shoot through in half an hour. Give the Joes a shout, and we'll go out and get her wound up.'

The navigator nodded, then rose and went to a door that gave access to an adjoining room. He tapped on the door first, then opened it a little and announced: 'It's on. Thirty minutes.'

In the next room, eight men regarded the door that closed behind the navigator with expressions that ranged from relief to resignation. Relief predominated, for it had been a long wait.

The eight men wore dark-coloured overalls. Each man carried a pack in which, as well as the necessary rations, was stowed the equipment that was suited to the individual task he had to perform. More gear was tucked away in their overall pockets. Each man also carried a sub-machine-gun, not of British design, but a German MP-40, preferred when operating inside enemy territory because the ammunition it used could be replenished from captured supplies.

It was four days since Douglas had reported to Montgomery's headquarters; four hectic days of briefings and organization, of cramming his small team with all the information that was necessary for carrying out the job in hand. Each man now knew the layout of Rommel's HQ as though it were his own back garden.

What it had not been possible to do was formulate a plan of attack. That would have to wait until they were in France, and in a position to make a first-hand reconnaissance.

Covertly, Douglas surveyed the other members of his team. Some had been with him since the early days in the desert, others had joined him since, but they had all seen action together. Some of them, he fancied, looked weary, although the waiting might account for that. The waiting was always the worst.

One man caught his gaze and winked at him, smiling. Douglas grinned back, thinking that it would take a great deal to perturb his second-in-command, Lieutenant Liam Conolly. The saturnine Irishman looked completely at ease, sitting on the floor with his back to the wall, his MP-40 resting across his knees.

Conolly was one of the originals. Conolly, the graduate of Dublin University, whose linguistic talents had got Douglas's small SAS team out of a potential mess on more than one occasion. Conolly, the irrepressible womanizer, each of his leaves bringing fresh complications. Douglas had often wondered how the women Conolly had bedded would react if they knew how many men had died under the hands that caressed them.

Troop Sergeant-Major Stan Brough was another original, a stocky, solid Yorkshireman whose life revolved round his wife, Edna, and their little home on the outskirts of York. Brough's sole purpose was to get his war over as quickly as possible, so that he could pick up the threads of his pre-war life on the railway. Douglas, however, had a small suspicion that deep down Brough had become attached to the army, and that he would find himself reluctant to leave it when peace came. If he did, the army would lose a first-rate, utterly dependable senior NCO, the kind of man that would be needed to hold it together when soldiering once again became a career of choice. Stan Brough was the kind of man who never raised his voice, except when on parade; he never needed to.

Another bird of similar feather was Troop Sergeant Brian Olds, the former Norfolk farm boy who had a unique ability to sniff out the secrets of the countryside like a hound. The flight of a bird, the scurrying of an animal, were enough to tell Olds where danger might lie. Unlike Brough, Olds had no desire to leave the army; the army had made him somebody, lifting him right out of the station in life where, it had been emphasised to him many times as a boy, he belonged. Well, Brian Olds had told himself, he was not going to be kicked around from pillar to post as his father had been, booted out of one tied cottage after another on the whim of some farmer. Olds had seen more of the world than all the Norfolk farmers put together. He would show them.

Olds' friend, Corporal Bill Mitchell, was a complete contrast. He was a Rhodesian, from one of that country's longest-established settler families. A taciturn, almost secretive man, he spoke mostly in monosyllables, as though conserving reserves of energy, which seemed inexhaustible. Mitchell was the detachment's signals specialist, and in many ways had the toughest job of all, for he had to carry a bulky radio set as well as his personal pack. Yet he could run up one side of a mountain and down the other with his load, with barely an increase in his heartbeat rate.

The other three members of the team were all SAS troopers: Lambert, Barber and Sansom. Barber was the explosives expert; a Cockney, he had lost his only relatives during the *Blitz* of 1940, and now took a great personal delight in sending the enemy sky-high with the various means at his disposal. Barber could concoct explosive devices out of almost anything, and use them to fearsome effect. The other two were there primarily to assist him in this task, although they had specialist skills of their own; Lambert, for example, was an expert safe-breaker, while Sansom's *forte* was tapping telephones. He was also expert with a crossbow.

Outside the cottage, the rain gave a last flurry, then pattered into silence. As the SAS men busied themselves with last-minute checks of their weapons and equipment, an aero-engine coughed throatily into life, followed by another, as the Hudson crew made their pre-flight preparations.

It was barely six months since Douglas and his men had last flown into France in a Hudson prior to their swift and effective attack on the enemy airfield at Istres, where missile-armed enemy bombers had threatened the passage of Allied convoys through the Mediterranean. On that occasion they had flown from Tempsford, in Bedfordshire, where the Hudsons, Lysanders and Halifaxes of the RAF's special duties squadrons were located; the RAF used Tangmere as an advance base for swift agent-dropping trips across the Channel.

The noise of the engines swelled to a roar as the pilot applied power, then died to a mutter as he throttled back to idling speed. A couple of minutes later the navigator re-appeared in the cottage and poked his head round the door where Douglas and his men were waiting. He had no idea who these men might be, but he had to admit that they were a tough-looking bunch. To him they were simply 'Joes', which was the nickname given by the crews of the black-painted aircraft to the men and women they carried to the continent on their secret assignments.

'All set,' he informed Douglas. 'Time to go.'

'Okay. Thanks.' Douglas stood up and nodded to the others, who followed him out into the darkness. It was just after 01.00 hours. The clouds had dispersed, their remnants scudding away to the north. The wind was fresh, and warmer than Douglas had expected. Stars glittered overhead.

The navigator waited as the eight SAS men climbed aboard the Hudson, then entered the aircraft himself and closed the fuselage hatch behind him, making sure that it was securely locked. As Douglas strapped himself into one of the canvas 'bucket' seats next to the metal wall of the fuselage, he wondered idly if this was the same aircraft that had taken them to France before. It would certainly be a shorter trip this time; the previous one had lasted four hours, most of it through severe turbulence, and they had all been violently airsick. There had been a third crew member then, too, a radio operator.

The navigator moved up the narrow aisle between the seats, his face ghostly in the light of a dim blue lamp overhead, and checked that the passengers' seat straps were secure. Then he went forward, tapped the pilot on the shoulder and settled himself at his position in the Hudson's glazed nose. Beside the aircraft's wings stood the shadowy forms of two airmen, holding ropes attached to the chocks in front of the Hudson's wheels. Their eyes were on the cockpit, waiting for the flash of the pilot's hand-torch that would be the signal to pull the chocks away.

The pilot called up the navigator on the intercom. 'Okay, George, give 'em the green.'

'Roger, skip.'

The navigator picked up an Aldis lamp and pointed it through the perspex in the direction of the control tower, which stood several hundred yards away. He pressed the trigger of the lamp and squeezed off a series of green flashes, the signal for clearance to taxi, anticipating a similar response. Instead, a continuous red light shone from the tower.

'We're getting a red, skip,' the navigator said urgently.

'I see it,' the pilot muttered. 'Now what the hell!'

A vehicle was approaching the aircraft from the direction of the control tower, driving straight across the grass and, to judge from the bouncing of its masked headlights, moving pretty fast. It slowed as it approached the Hudson and came to a halt near the wingtip. Someone got out and walked quickly to the fuselage hatch. There was a thumping sound.

'You forgot to let the cat in, George. Nip back and see what's what,' the pilot said.

Grumbling, the navigator unfastened his straps and made his way back through the cabin. He unlocked the hatch, opened it, and a bulky figure scrambled in. The newcomer spoke a few urgent words into the navigator's ear.

'Better come up front and see the skipper,' the navigator said. 'But make it quick.'

The SAS men looked up in curiosity as the dim shape hurried past them, heading for the flight-deck. A couple of minutes later it returned, minus the navigator, and dropped into a spare bucket seat behind Douglas. Whoever it was, Douglas noticed, seemed to be wearing civilian clothing, although it was hard to tell in the dim light of the cabin.

The car that had brought the new passenger went back the way it had come. The navigator flashed his Aldis again, and this time received an intermittent green light in reply.

'Steer two-zero-zero after take-off, skip,' he instructed.

The flight plan called for the Hudson to fly a big dog-leg out to a point beyond the Channel Islands. It would then turn due east across the Gulf of St Malo, making landfall near Granville and crossing Normandy to the rear of the formidable German coastal flak defences. Its eventual destination, after a flight of 140 miles inland from the coast, was a large field to the east of Evreux. At no point, except to avoid rising ground, would the aircraft fly higher than one thousand feet above sea level.

The Hudson rumbled out to its take-off point. A steady green light shone from the control tower and the pilot opened the throttles slowly, running the engines up to full power. The aircraft began to move as he released the brakes, gathering speed in the darkness. The tail came up and the rumbling ceased as the Hudson lifted into the air. The pilot held the aircraft level until it reached the safe flying speed, then retracted the undercarriage and turned carefully on to the course his navigator had given him. Minutes later, the Hudson was passing over the Isle of Wight and heading out over the Channel.

The pilot breathed a sigh of relief once he was well out over the sea. He disliked flying anywhere near Portsmouth. The port was heavily defended, and although the defences had been warned of the aircraft's departure, the Navy had a habit of blasting off at anything, no matter in which direction it was flying.

In the cabin, Douglas was relieved too. So far, there had been no savage air pockets to make his stomach heave. The Hudson's engines drummed with a comfortable, unfaltering beat.

A sudden tap on the back startled him. He released his

restraining seat belt and looked over his shoulder. It took his eyes a moment to focus, and when they did his mouth dropped open.

Even in the dim cabin lighting, there was no mistaking the face that peered short-sightedly at him from beneath a floppy Frenchman's beret. It belonged to Major Walter Fitzroy.

'Good God!' Douglas cried over the noise of the engines. 'What the blazes are you doing here?'

Fitzroy leaned forward, placing his mouth close to Douglas's ear so that he could make himself heard without shouting loudly.

'Last minute orders, old boy. There's trouble. I'm not here by choice. Monty sent me.'

'What sort of trouble?' Douglas asked, alarmed.

'I'll be as brief as I can,' Fitzroy promised. 'About three weeks ago, we landed a small group of Commandos – two officers and three men – on the Normandy coast. Their task was to work their way inland and carry out a reconnaissance of possible approach routes to Rommel's HQ. They came ashore from a Folboat – you know, those collapsible canoes – having been dropped by a submarine, and the sub was to have picked them up ten days later. The trouble was, they didn't turn up at the rendezvous.'

'Why wasn't I told about this?' Douglas asked truculently.

'Because they had no bearing on your mission unless they returned with the necessary information,' Fitzroy said hastily. 'We've been hanging on in the hope that they would turn up. You know, they could have got held up somehow. Anything could have happened.'

He paused, then went on slowly: 'Well, now we've an inkling of what did happen. Mind you, it's only an inkling – we've no real information. We think they may have been picked up by the enemy.'

There was an even longer pause. Then Douglas asked: 'How much did they know? About our mission, I mean?'

'Not a great deal, except . . . except that they were to have been put in touch with the Resistance cell. The one you are supposed to make rendezvous with. They were to have been passed from one Resistance group to another, you see, as they crossed Normandy behind enemy lines.'

'Go on,' Douglas said, his tone grim.

'Well, our worry is if they have been picked up, they might have talked under pressure. They didn't know anything about you – I want to assure you of that – only that they were to carry out a recce. But if they were caught anywhere near Rommel's HQ, it wouldn't take the Germans long to put two and two together. And, of course, the Resistance people might have been compromised.'

Compromised, Douglas thought. A nice word, but hardly one descriptive of being tortured half to death, then put up against a wall and shot.

'And if they have been *compromised*, as you put it,' he said, placing emphasis on the word, 'this whole operation might be in jeopardy. Damn it, I'm not risking the lives of my men on a fool's errand! I'm for calling it off.'

'Can't do that, old boy,' Fitzroy told him firmly. 'Far too much at stake. The operation goes ahead. We haven't heard from the Resistance cell for forty-eight hours,' he admitted, 'but if the hunt is up that could well be a security precaution. Whatever happens, your job is still to bump off Rommel. Mine is to find out for certain what has happened to the Commandos. I'd rather not be here, you know.'

Fitzroy lapsed back into his seat. He had told Douglas so much, but there was more – a great deal more, and all of it knowledge that would be dangerous for the SAS officer to possess, if the worst should happen.

The Hudson droned on. It was by no means the only aircraft airborne over the Channel that night, but only one other was on a mission closely connected with its own.

For the past two hours, a twin-engined Douglas Havoc night-fighter had been cruising in broad circles over the sea at twenty thousand feet, midway between Start Point and the Channel Islands. The Havoc, in fact, was no longer used as a night-fighter, having been replaced in that role by the far more deadly de Havilland Mosquito. Most of the remaining

Havocs had now been stripped of their guns and radar equipment and were used for other duties.

The one now circling over the Channel, with an intensely bored crew of three on board, was one of a pair based at Predannack, in Cornwall. Taking off in squally rain, it had climbed through the clouds into clear skies. Pale blue fires of static electricity played among the strange aerials that festooned the underside of its fuselage.

In the darkened rear of the cockpit, the radio operator crouched over his equipment, listening intently. If previous nights were anything to go by, he would be out of luck on this occasion, too. These so-called 'Ascension' sorties were becoming a bore. Although the idea behind them was sound enough, it seldom produced results in practice.

The Havoc was in fact an airborne relay station. The radio operator's job was to pick up very high frequency voice transmissions from agents in occupied Europe, and relay them to stations in England or to special duties aircraft en route across the Channel. In theory, the technique enabled agents to use man-portable equipment to transmit their messages, avoiding the need to set up equipment for transmitting Morse Code, which could be easily detected and pinpointed by the enemy.

The voice sounded in the radio operator's earphones unexpectedly, fighting its way faintly through the fuzz of static. The voice was repeating a string of code-words, over and over.

The wireless operator scribbled the words down on a pad at his elbow and turned up the dimmer switch, strengthening the light above his small table. He leafed through the pages of a code book, running his gloved finger down a column.

'Christ,' he muttered. 'That's torn it.'

Reaching out, he turned the dial on his radio transmitter until it registered a certain frequency. He pressed the transmit switch and spoke into his microphone.

'Nan Able Baker, abort, abort. Nan Able Baker, abort.'

He repeated the message several times, then he closed down his station and spoke to the pilot over the intercom.

'All right, skipper, that's it. We can go home now.'

The pilot glanced at his fuel gauges, relaxed and gave a large yawn. 'Thank Christ for that,' he said gratefully.

As radio silence was of paramount importance, the radio operator in the Havoc had not expected the pilot of the Hudson, flying nineteen thousand feet lower down somewhere off the Channel Islands, to pass an acknowledgement of his urgent message, and so he was not surprised when none came.

The Hudson, meanwhile, droned steadily on. The pilot took it in a broad sweep around the Channel Islands, picking up the Normandy coast exactly at the spot where a wide river estuary led inland towards the ancient town of Coutances. The coastal defences were silent, which rather surprised the pilot; there was usually some flak to be expected.

Directly ahead of the Hudson's nose, the tired, pale sliver of the waning moon rose above the horizon. On the ground, a few pinpricks of light gleamed here and there, provoking a comment from the navigator.

'Bloody awful blackout, as usual.'

The pilot grunted a reply. Privately, he was convinced that ordinary French folk, risking imprisonment or worse, deliberately showed lights from their cottages when they heard an Allied aircraft pass overhead; British and American aero-engines did not sound the same as German ones, and were easily distinguishable.

The pilot did not like these midsummer night sorties, with only a few hours of darkness between sunset and sunrise. Even assuming that he made the drop quickly and without trouble, it would be growing light by the time the Hudson re-crossed the French coast on its homeward leg, and even if the aircraft negotiated the coastal flak defences successfully, there was always the risk that it might run into a dawn patrol of Focke-Wulfs over the Channel. The only consolation was that the enemy fighter defences were thinly stretched, many fighter squadrons having been withdrawn for the defence of Germany, or sent to the Russian front.

The navigator, map-reading in the nose, announced that

the river Orne was ahead. The Hudson crossed it a couple of minutes later to the north of Falaise, climbing to 1,500 feet above sea level to give it a safe height over the wooded slopes to the east of the river.

'Anything from Ascension, skipper?' the navigator asked. The question caused the pilot to frown. He suddenly realized that there had been no static in his headphones for some time. It was at times like this that he wished they still carried a wireless operator, instead of dispensing with him to make room for an extra passenger if need be. The radio installation had been modified so that it could be operated by the pilot, and it had turned out to be an unfortunate compromise.

He reached out and fiddled with the frequency selector for a few moments, turning up the volume. There was still no sound in his headphones.

'Bloody radio's packed in,' he announced in disgust. 'That's the third time in a month.' The pilot hated having an unserviceable radio. It meant that if they ran into trouble over the Channel, on the way home, he would not be able to summon help.

In the nose, the navigator shrugged resignedly and concentrated on his map reading, using rivers as his main guide. He had flown this route several times already, and was familiar with the contours of the darkened land. Even so, he needed all his wits about him.

Suddenly, the northern sky erupted in brilliance. The horizon flickered with light and the thin, pencil-like beams of searchlights probed into the sky.

'Where's that, George?' the pilot asked.

'Must be twenty miles off,' the navigator answered. 'Looks like Le Havre.'

The distant firework display lasted for several minutes. The pilot glanced at it from time to time, in between checking the course he was steering and his altitude. Once, he saw a pinprick of light appear near a searchlight cone, flare into brilliance and then fade as it dropped slowly down the sky.

'Some poor sod's bought it,' he muttered to himself. The sight brought a sick feeling to his stomach. His last operation with Bomber Command, before being posted at his own request to special duties operations, had been to Nuremberg on the last night of March 1944. He and his crew had survived, but ninety-five other crews had not. The sight of burning Lancasters and Halifaxes, falling in flames from the night sky one after the other, was something that would live with him until the day he died.

In the aircraft's nose, the navigator spotted a thin plume of steam up ahead and nodded in satisfaction. A train, he thought, heading along the railway line between Lisieux and Bernay. He could see the line now, or rather the dark gash it made in the terrain. A small river, gleaming palely in the moonlight, ran alongside it.

In a few more moments, the Hudson would be over the spot where the line divided, one branch heading north towards the coast, the other south to Conches and, eventually, to Paris.

'Stand by, skipper,' he instructed. 'Turning point coming up in thirty seconds. New heading is one-four-five. Fifteen seconds . . . now!'

The pilot pulled the Hudson round tightly, the sudden turn startling the occupants in the cabin, some of whom had been dozing. He levelled the wings again and looked down to his left, through the side panel of the cockpit. He was flying over a flat plain now, and the dark slash of the railway line was clearly visible. He throttled back slightly, reducing the flying speed, and turned his attention to the view through the windscreen.

In his nose position, the navigator was counting off the seconds. This was the nerve-racking part, the final approach to the objective – a field with a few dim lights that designated their flarepath.

'Turn left ninety degrees – now!'

The pilot turned the control column and re-opened the throttles a little, anxious not to lose airspeed in the turn. In the cabin, Douglas, aware that they would soon be landing, passed the word among his men to tighten their seat straps and have their equipment handy, ready for a rapid exit. They did not really need to be told; all of them, with the exception of Fitzroy, had travelled to France by this means before.

'I've got the lights, skipper,' the navigator said urgently. 'Ten degrees to starboard.'

'Okay, I see them. Well done, George.' The lights were laid out in the shape of a large L, the smaller arm of the L denoting the downwind edge of the landing field. As the wind was from the south-west, the pilot would have to fly past the field and then turn in for his landing from the direction of Evreux. There was a German airfield at Saint André, not far away, so with luck the enemy would think that the Hudson was an intruder aircraft, cruising in the neighbourhood in the hope of catching a night-flying German aircraft. Saint André was a bomber base, and had received a good deal of attention from the RAF's Mosquitos.

Keeping the dim, improvised lights of the flarepath in sight all the while, the pilot lowered his undercarriage and flaps and brought the Hudson round in a steady turn until he was heading directly for the short arm of the L. He kept one hand on the throttles, using all his concentration to ensure that he touched down as close to the boundary of the field as possible. Sometimes, these secret landing grounds were barely larger than a football pitch.

A torch flickered at him from the ground, as someone at the far end of the landing strip flashed an identification letter. The navigator saw it too, and his shout over the intercom was deafening.

'Skipper, it's a trap! Pull up! PULL UP!'

Suddenly, the pilot knew what the navigator meant. The code letter being flashed by hand torch was correct; its colour was not. The identification letters flashed to incoming RAF aircraft by the Resistance were always red, the necessary colour usually achieved by holding a piece of red paper over the torch.

This one was yellow.

Adrenalin pumping, the pilot pushed open the throttles. The Hudson's two Wright Cyclone engines howled in response and the nose rose steeply as he eased back the control column, at the same time raising the undercarriage and flaps.

The next instant, the Hudson was flying through a storm of machine-gun fire. Bullets tore through the wings and fuselage, luckily without hitting anyone inside. The pilot stood the aircraft on its wingtip, narrowly missing a line of trees in his frantic efforts to escape the murderous fire. Levelling out, he brought the Hudson down as low as he dared, skimming over treetops and power lines.

The gunfire died away astern. The pilot's hands were sticky on the control column, and sweat poured into his eyes.

"Strewth, that was close! You okay, George?'

The navigator's breathless reply came over the intercom. 'Yeah, I think so . . . There's a hell of a draught in here, though. A bullet went through the perspex and just missed my head.'

'Better go back and tell the Joes what's happened,' the pilot said. 'They're probably crapping themselves.'

Grateful for the chance to stretch his legs, the navigator wormed his way out of the nose position and went back into the cabin. The pilot continued to head due west, the pale glow of the moon reflected in his rear-view mirror.

Moments later, the glow of the moon was eclipsed by a bright orange flash that lit up the cockpit. Heart in mouth, the pilot looked out along the starboard wing. A streamer of flame, fanned by the propeller's slipstream, was whirling back from the engine.

Acting instinctively, he shut down the burning engine, punched the fire extinguisher button and operated the lever that 'feathered' the propeller, turning the windmilling blades edge-on to the airflow to cut down their drag. The fire continued unchecked, the flames now eating their way hungrily across the wing towards the fuel tank. He knew that he had a couple of minutes, maybe less, before the tank exploded and tore the wing off.

The crippled aircraft was beginning to lose height. The

ground was rushing up. He had no idea what lay below, and no time to warn his passengers. All he could do was keep the wings level as the Hudson sank lower. In a last, despairing gesture, he dropped full flap to reduce the airspeed.

The blazing aircraft hit the ground just short of a minor road. As it struck, the burning wing hit a telegraph pole and ripped away, scattering liquid fire in all directions. The remainder of the aircraft tore through a tall hedge, which slowed its progress considerably, and slewed violently into a meadow. It pitched up on its nose and, for a sickening instant, seemed certain to crash over on its back before crunching to earth the right way up.

The impact was terrific. In the rear of the cabin, Douglas's last coherent impression was of the luckless navigator's body hurtling down the catwalk to smash itself against the forward fuselage bulkhead.

Then there was only darkness.

CHAPTER FOUR

Douglas opened his eyes slowly. The lids seemed to be gummed together, and as he worked his facial muscles, forcing the reluctant lids apart, a lance of pain shot through his head. He closed the partly-open eyes quickly.

He tried to move, and could not. His arms and legs were leaden, devoid of feeling and completely immobile. He could only just move his neck, but the fearful pain in his head soon brought a halt to that attempt.

'Major Douglas is showing signs of life, I see.'

The words, delivered in a cultured English accent, startled Douglas out of the incipient panic that threatened to seize him. He forced his eyes open again, and this time succeeded in keeping them open, although he gasped audibly at the pain caused by the light that flooded into them. He perceived that it was bright sunlight, streaming almost horizontally through an open window. Beyond it, birds were singing.

His senses told him that he was lying on his back, on some sort of bed that was neither soft nor unduly hard. The atmosphere smelt of antiseptic fluid, and he deduced that he was probably in hospital. His arms were stretched out at right angles to his body, and as he rolled his head painfully from side to side he saw that they were strapped to the metal bed frame. So, although he could not see them without raising his head, must be his legs.

He looked for the source of the voice, and it was some

seconds before his eyes focused on it. A man was standing by the window, looking down at him. He wore an elegantly-cut black uniform, with the silver insignia of the ss on his collar. He was tall, fair haired, and deeply tanned. One arm rested on the window ledge; around the cuff was a band with the words *Prinz Eugen* embroidered on it in silver.

The man straightened up and walked slowly across the room to stand beside the bed. He smiled at Douglas in friendly fashion.

'Please forgive the straps, Major Douglas,' he said. 'They were necessary in case you had convulsions and fell out of bed, hurting yourself even more. You have received a very severe blow on the head. I will now have them removed.'

He went quickly to a door in the opposite wall, opened it and rapped out an order. Two men in white overalls stepped respectfully past him and approached the bed. They bent down, unfastened the straps that held Douglas in place, and raised him carefully to a sitting position, propping him up with pillows. His whole body agonized, as though he had been kicked half to death.

'There, now,' the ss officer said soothingly. 'That feels better, does it not?'

It did not, but Douglas didn't say so. His mind was having difficulty coming to terms with his situation. He reached up an exploratory hand, touching his head with his fingertips. There was a bulky bandage around it.

The ss officer said something in German to the two orderlies, who left the room, closing the door behind him.

'They will bring some soup presently,' he told Douglas. 'Meanwhile, perhaps you would like a glass of water.' He poured some liquid into a glass from a jug that stood on a little bedside table and handed it to Douglas. The latter, suddenly conscious of a raging thirst, gulped it down.

'Thanks,' he said, setting the tumbler down on the table. The ss Officer nodded. He clicked his heels and made a small bow.

'Von Radusch,' he said by way of introduction, at the same time making the name sound so much like the familiar root that it was all Douglas could do to refrain from laughing, despite his

discomfort. Instead, he kept a straight face and compli-
mented the ss officer on his excellent English.

'My mother was English,' von Radusch explained. 'I went
to Oxford before the war.'

'Oh, really?' Douglas said. 'I'm afraid I didn't.'

The German smiled. 'I know that, Major. In fact, I know a
great deal about you. Why you are here, for example.'

'I wish I knew that,' Douglas said. 'I can't recall anything.
Bang on the head, you said?'

There was some truth in the statement. When he came
round, Douglas had been able to remember taking off from
England, and nothing more. Fragments were only now
beginning to come back to him. He decided to play dumb and
let von Radusch do the talking. He would stick to the old
'name, rank and number' routine.

'You received a nasty gash in your scalp,' the German said,
'but no other serious injury. Just some bruising. You had a
very lucky escape. Quite miraculous, really; you were thrown
clear of the wreck.'

'Wreck? What wreck?' Flames and noise. The rending of
metal. A body hurtling through the air. Darkness.

Von Radusch smiled at him again. 'Oh, come now, Major.
You must remember. You were in an aircraft. It crashed. You
were the only survivor. All your friends are dead, I'm afraid.'

The most awful sickness, the most terrible dread Douglas
had ever experienced came over him then. Brough, Conolly,
Olds . . . all the others. Wiped out. Just like that. The
sickness lasted a few seconds, and was replaced by a numb
coldness. He looked up at von Radusch; the German's
expression gave no indication that he might be lying.

'I don't remember anything,' Douglas persisted. He had to
know more. Somehow, he had to persuade the German to
part with more information.

At that moment, one of the orderlies returned with the
promised soup on a tray, which he laid across Douglas's
thighs. Von Radusch made a gesture.

'Eat,' he said. 'We shall talk some more when you have
finished.' He went back to the window and stood gazing out

46

while Douglas stared moodily at the bowl in front of him. It contained clear soup, with some chunks of crusty bread floating in it. Douglas picked up the spoon and forced the food down; it stuck in his throat, but he knew that he had to digest it in order to regain some strength. He felt weak, probably through the blood lost from his head wound, and he had no idea when his next meal might be.

He took his time over finishing the soup, chewing each fragment of bread carefully. At length, he set the tray aside on the table and waited for what was going to come next. He felt uncomfortable and at a disadvantage, because he was completely naked except for a rough army blanket that lay across him. He wondered what had become of his special overall.

Von Radusch, seeing that Douglas had finished his meal, drew a chair up to the bedside and sat astride it, his arms folded on the back. He stared at the captive for a few moments, then said quickly:

'Forget any notions of trying to escape, Major. There are armed guards outside that window, and more in the corridor. They have orders to shoot you dead if you try anything. Besides, think of the indignity of being shot with no clothes on.'

He paused and produced a silver cigarette case, offering Douglas its contents. Douglas declined; the German took a cigarette himself, inserted it into a short holder and lit it. He blew a thin stream of smoke over Douglas's head and said seriously:

'You know that you stand in grave danger of being shot? The *Führer* has issued a directive on how you Commando gangsters are to be treated.'

So the true colours are being flown at last, Douglas thought. 'I'm not a gangster,' he said. 'And what makes you think I'm a Commando?'

Von Radusch smiled tolerantly. 'As I told you, Major, we know a great deal about you.' He tapped his cigarette holder, and ash fell on to the floor.

'Who gave you the order to assassinate Field Marshal Rommel?' he asked out of the blue. 'Was it Montgomery, or Eisenhower himself? I should have thought that the order

47

might have come directly from Eisenhower, as he is the Supreme Allied Commander, but we all know that Monty rather resents Ike being in charge. Perhaps Monty wants to stage a coup, so that he can get into the limelight?' Coming from the German's lips, the Allied commanders' nicknames sounded incongruous.

Douglas shrugged. 'I haven't a clue what you're talking about. Look. I've just about had enough of this. Where are my clothes? I want to get up.'

The German put out a restraining hand. 'All in good time. When you have answered some questions. It will be better to answer them now, Major, because some of our interrogators are by no means as tolerant as myself. Now, is it not true that you were briefed to kill Rommel on the eve of your invasion?'

Douglas was taken aback at the depth of the German's knowledge, and hoped that he did not show it. But his expression must have given something away, because von Radusch chuckled.

'Yes, Major, we know the invasion is coming, and we also know where the landings will take place. It will be good to see the British and Americans put up a proper fight for once, before we utterly destroy them.'

'They don't seem to have been doing too badly so far,' Douglas grunted. 'What about North Africa? And Italy?'

'Bah!' Von Radusch's tone was contemptuous. 'North Africa was a sideshow, nothing more. We were only forced to withdraw because of a lack of supplies. And as for Italy – well, the less said about the Italians the better. It was mostly their fault we had problems in North Africa in the first place.'

He wagged a finger at Douglas. 'The Russian front, now – that's a different story. The Russians know how to fight.'

'Obviously,' Douglas said mildly. 'I gather you are coming second.'

Von Radusch's face suddenly darkened and his voice became curt. 'Enough! I am not here to discuss the conduct of the war with you.'

'Good,' Douglas said. 'Now perhaps you'll tell me where I am, give me my clothes back and send me off to a prison camp. You might as well, because I'm damned if you are going to get anything out of me other than my name and rank, which you know already.'

He closed his eyes. His head was hurting abominably, possibly because the effects of some local anaesthetic were wearing off, and for the first time the grim news about his men was really beginning to sink in. As reaction began to affect him, he felt an overwhelming sense of despair and failure.

Wearily, he opened his eyes, only half-listening as von Radusch spoke again.

'Soon I will let you rest for a while,' he said. 'But first I have a little surprise for you – something that might help to jog your ailing memory.'

He got up and left the room abruptly. Douglas waited for a few seconds after the door closed and then threw aside the blanket, swinging his legs out of bed. His head reeled and he was forced to sit still for several moments; then, with an enormous effort, he heaved himself upright, balancing with one hand on the bedside table. Finding his balance, he reached down for the blanket, which he draped around himself toga-fashion, and made his way unsteadily to the open window.

Outside, the morning sun shone brightly through the branches of tall elms. The hospital, if such it was, seemed to be set in some sort of park. In the distance, Douglas could see a high wall, and beyond that the spires and towers of what looked like a cathedral. He made a mental note of that; it might give him a clue to the place's identity.

A shaft of sunlight gleamed on dull metal, causing him to look down. The room in which he was held prisoner was on the first floor, facing one of the larger trees. By its trunk a German soldier stood, cradling a machine-pistol.

He gazed up at Douglas and patted the weapon suggestively. Douglas stuck two fingers up at him and returned to his bed.

After a while, he heard the tramp of feet in the corridor outside his room. Steel-shod boots crashed to a halt. The door was flung open and von Radusch came in, pushing someone before him.

Douglas stared, his face a mask, his heart in the grip of ice. There were bruises on the face of von Radusch's captive; her hair, sweat-stained and bedraggled, hung lankly down either side of her face.

Colette stared back at him with dead eyes, and gave no sign of recognition.

'A touching reunion,' von Radusch said. 'Is there to be no greeting between you? A little kiss on the cheek, perhaps?'

He pushed Colette sharply towards the bed. She stumbled, and barely managed to right herself. Douglas saw that her hands were tied behind her back.

His own hands twitched on the blanket. He wanted nothing more than to fasten them round von Radusch's throat, to crush his larynx to pulp. The German read the hatred in his eyes and rested the palm of his right hand on the butt of a pistol in a holster at his side. He had not been wearing it before.

'So, we have a reaction, after all,' he said softly. He gave Colette another shove and she collapsed face down at the foot of the bed, across Douglas's legs. She turned her face slightly towards him. It was hidden from von Radusch's view. Light had returned to her eyes, and in them Douglas read a single unspoken word: NO!

He looked at the German. 'I don't know what the hell you're playing at,' he protested. 'Who is this woman, and why have you brought her here?'

The tolerant smile vanished from von Radusch's face. 'Oh, come now, Major. You are beginning to annoy me. I told you that we know all about you; we also know all about this woman. Your fiancée,' he added.

Douglas's mind raced. One shock was piling on top of another, and it was almost more than he could take. He looked down at Colette again. What had they done to her?

Von Radusch moved around the end of the bed and crossed to the window, leaning against the sill. His finger-tips caressed the butt of the pistol as he gazed at Douglas. As though reading the SAS officer's thoughts, he said:

'Don't worry. She hasn't been harmed – yet. A few bruises don't matter. They're nothing. What *might* happen to her is something entirely different. As a matter of fact, one of her Resistance colleagues is in the room next door, enjoying a pleasant chat with some friends of mine. Unfortunately for him, it will soon cease to be pleasant.'

The German consulted his wrist watch. 'I am going to be generous, Major. I shall give you five minutes in which to collect your thoughts. Then I want you to tell me everything you know. Everything about your mission, everything about the organization to which you belong. Your girl-friend's life depends on it; so, perhaps, does the life of the unfortunate fellow next door.'

'Look,' Douglas snapped. 'I've told you. I don't remember anything. What's more, I've never set eyes on this woman. You won't get anything out of me, because I can't tell you anything.'

'Four minutes,' von Radusch said mildly.

A terrible scream, barely recognizable as coming from a human being, sounded from the adjoining room, scarcely muffled by the intervening wall. On the bed, Colette moan-ed softly.

Douglas moved his feet gently, trying to extricate them from beneath her body. He was calculating whether he had sufficient strength and agility to leap from the bed and get his hands on von Radusch before the latter had a chance to draw his pistol. Again, the German seemed to read his mind.

'It would be a waste of time, Major. You would be dead before you had taken two steps. And then I would take great pleasure in killing the woman. Slowly,' he said mean-ingfully.

More awful shrieks tore through the air, mingled with the sound of sobbing.

'The genitals,' von Radusch commented. 'They always scream like that, when we start on the genitals. Despite what you might believe, it is especially painful for the women. You have two minutes.'

Douglas continued to ease his feet from under Colette. At last they were clear. He was going to take a chance. Legs drawn carefully under him, ready for a sideways spring and a roll across the floor. Maybe he could distract von Radusch's aim – perhaps he could get a hand on the water jug and flick it across the room as he made his move.

'One minute.'

More terrible screams. It had to be now. A little smile played around von Radusch's lips. His hand now hung loosely beside the holster, as though he were keen to test the speed of his draw.

There was a sudden, sharp sound, like a cricket bat striking leather. Von Radusch rose to his full height, and the smile vanished from his face. His right hand fluttered briefly. Then he toppled like a felled tree, crashing face down on the floor to lie twitching.

A crossbow bolt protruded from the back of his head.

Douglas flung himself out of bed and stepped over the fallen man. Cautiously, he peered out of the window. The first thing he saw was Sansom, crossbow in hand, standing in the shade of the big tree astride the corpse of the German sentry.

Then he saw a second man, standing immediately below the window, looking up at him.

'For Christ's sake, Boss, get a move on!' Conolly said. 'We haven't much time!'

CHAPTER FIVE

Douglas ripped at the cords that secured Colette's wrists. His fingers were shaking, and it took him half a minute before he could get them undone. She was sobbing. Her arms free, she turned and clutched him to her, her face pressed against his chest.

Roughly, he disengaged himself. 'Come on, love. Bear up. We've got to get away from here. Give me a hand, will you?'

She brushed away her tears, regained some composure and set about helping Douglas to strip off the dead German's tunic and trousers. Quickly, he put them on, then forced his feet with difficulty into von Radusch's boots. They were a size too small. As a final act, he buckled the German's belt, complete with holster and gun, around his waist.

He stuck his head out of the window. Below, Conolly beckoned frantically to him. Douglas gestured to Colette.

'Come on! You first. I'll hold on to you.'

So far, Colette had not spoken a word. She moved automatically, as though in shock. She wore slacks and a woollen pullover, torn at the shoulder.

She climbed over the window sill and hung on. Douglas grasped her by the wrists, angrily noticing the marks of the ropes that had bound her as he did so, and leaned forward, lowering her to the full extent of her arms so that Conolly could grasp her and swing her to the ground. Then he followed suit, letting go and dropping the last few feet. The

53

shock of the landing sent another stab of pain through his injured head.

Conolly reached out to steady him, then urged Douglas and Colette towards the shelter of the trees. Sansom had dragged the body of the German guard into some bushes.

'We're heading for the wall, over there,' Conolly said, pointing to a spot between a pair of elms. He looked at Douglas and Colette in turn. 'Can you run?' he asked.

'Yes. I'm all right,' Colette said, speaking for the first time. Douglas nodded.

'Let's go, then. We've got friends on the other side. But we must be quick – this place will be wide awake shortly.'

'It's probably wide awake already,' Douglas panted as they zigzagged between the trees, his head throbbing. 'They were torturing some poor beggar in there. He was screaming fit to bring the house down.'

'I don't suppose anyone would take much notice,' Conolly answered. 'It's a lunatic asylum.'

Douglas saw that both Conolly and Sansom were wearing rough French peasant clothing. He felt completely out of control of his own destiny; this was all some dreadful dream, and he would wake up in a minute. His head was beginning to swim.

They reached the wall. A rope ladder was draped over it. 'Up you go, Sambo,' the Irishman said to Sansom, 'and make sure the coast is clear. There's a cart full of hay on the other side,' he explained to the other two. 'As soon as you're over, bury yourselves in it as far as you can and keep quiet. Explanations later.'

Sansom scrambled up to the top of the wall, announced that all was clear and dropped out of sight. Colette followed him, and then Douglas, with Conolly bringing up the rear. The Irishman pulled up the rope ladder after him.

It was a short drop into the hay. A horse stood patiently between the shafts, its head bowed, and a man, also in the garb of a French peasant, sat at the front of the cart. He turned his head as Douglas descended and winked. It was Fitzroy.

The others burrowed their way into the hay and lay there breathlessly, dust stinging their nostrils. Up front, Fitzroy tapped the horse's buttocks with a long stick and clicked his tongue. The cart jolted into movement.

Douglas lay with his face close to Colette's. She stared at him wide-eyed in the semi-darkness. He reached out carefully and stroked her cheek; she moved her hand and clasped his. The horse's hooves clopped steadily.

Perched on the cart, Fitzroy tried not to sweat and to appear nonchalant, playing out his role. The horse appeared to know exactly where it was going, and for this he was grateful; although he had been given exact directions, it would have been all too easy to make a mistake. A fatal mistake, under the present circumstances.

The cart trundled on through ancient streets. A few townspeople were up and about, but not many. An elderly woman, carrying a basket of vegetables, called out a greeting as the cart passed her; Fitzroy returned it, doffing his beret courteously. He noted thankfully that no German patrols were in evidence, but he had already learned that the people in these parts did not go out of their way to cause trouble. In fact, many of the menfolk were working on the German coastal fortifications, making a great deal of money in Occupation currency – and quietly passing on information about the defences to others who knew how to make good use of it.

The cart passed through a square. There was an ornamental fountain in the centre, and on one side stood an elaborately sculptured clock tower. There was an archway beneath it, fenced off by spiked iron railings. The archway partly concealed a field gun, its barrel pointing up at an angle; it was a 75-millimetre, the famous *soixante quinze*, doubtless placed there as a memento of the Great War.

After a while, the patient carthorse turned into a side street with timber-fronted houses on either side. At the far end was a courtyard. The horse pricked up its ears, whinnied, and increased its plodding pace slightly.

This, Fitzroy knew from the description that had been

given to him, was the place. He pulled on the reins, drawing up the horse in the centre of the courtyard, and waited anxiously, looking round. There were rows of split stable doors on two sides of the yard, with horses' heads protruding from the top halves of some. The animals were hunters, and thoroughbreds at that. On the other side of the yard there was a big double door, with a bar across it.

After a minute or two, one of the stable doors opened and a young man emerged. He was small and wiry, darkly complexioned, and wore a baggy shirt and riding breeches. He carried some items of harness, draped around his shoulders.

The young man came up to the cart and looked up at Fitzroy. He smiled, showing brilliant white teeth, and extended his right hand. Fitzroy leaned down and shook it.

'I am Marc,' the man said. He nodded towards the cart. 'You have brought the whole consignment?'

'Not all,' Fitzroy told him. 'Some remains at the farm.'

'No matter,' Marc said. 'We will unload what you have brought.'

He went across to the double door and unbarred it, swinging the two halves wide open, and indicated that Fitzroy was to take the horse and cart inside. As soon as they were safely under cover, he closed the doors again.

Fitzroy turned and addressed the pile of hay behind him. 'All right, Callum. You can come out now.'

Douglas, Colette and the others appeared from their hiding place and stepped down from the cart, looking around them in curiosity. Marc shook the hands of each in turn, and appeared to treat Colette with considerable deference.

Light entered the storehouse – for such it was – through a pair of small windows, set high in the wall. Fitzroy held a conversation in French with Marc, then turned to Douglas.

'He's going to see to the unloading of the hay,' he said, 'and then I'm going back for the others. I'll be all right – my papers are immaculate. In the meantime, you'll be quite safe here.' He grinned suddenly. 'Nowadays, the stables are used mainly by German officers. It's the last place anyone would think of looking for you. With any luck you won't be here for very long, anyway.'

While Marc set about forking hay from the cart and stacking it in a pile in one corner of the storehouse, Douglas drew his party to one side.

'First of all,' he said, 'you'd better tell me what's been going on. You're all supposed to be dead.'

He looked at Colette, who was sitting on some bags of grain. 'I had a feeling you might be mixed up in all this somehow,' he told her. He had not yet recovered from the shock of seeing her, and was having trouble in analyzing his sentiments.

She opened her mouth to speak, but Conolly interrupted her. 'Well, we are alive, as you can see. We thought *you* must be dead. Most of us were knocked out stone cold in the crash, and when we came round it was absolute bedlam. The navigator was killed – as you know, he wasn't strapped in when the 'plane hit the ground – and so was the pilot. Pity about that; he did a hell of a job getting us down, but the cockpit was bashed up in the impact.

'Anyway,' he went on, 'we gradually pulled ourselves together. Apart from some cuts and bruises we were all okay, which was pretty miraculous, as the fuselage had split in two. It was when we started looking for you that we had a problem. You weren't there.'

Douglas closed his eyes. His hand moved involuntarily towards the bandage on his head. 'I don't remember anything after the crash,' he said. 'The next thing I knew, I was in a hospital bed with an ss officer for company.'

'Well, you weren't thrown out,' Conolly said, 'because we had a good look around the wreck. I think you must have wandered off and fallen down somewhere. We couldn't search any longer, because we saw some lights in the distance, heading our way fast. We headed for the nearest woods and kept going. It was Major Fitzroy who really saved our bacon; he went off and found a local farmer, who turned out to be friendly.'

A thought struck Douglas. 'How long ago was all this?' he asked. Conolly seemed surprised.

'Why, the day before yesterday. It's the third of June.'

'Good God!' Douglas felt unutterably weary. 'How did you find out where I was?'

It was Fitzroy who answered. 'That was a stroke of luck. One of the farmer's neighbours delivers eggs to the asylum. He came back with the news that a survivor of the 'plane crash had been taken there. We knew that it could only be you. We also learned that two or three members of the Resistance were being held there for questioning.'

Douglas looked at Colette. He wished that he could feel something for her, except for concern and dismay that she was here. She seemed almost a stranger, remote from him.

'Colette,' he said, 'do you feel like telling us what happened?'

She gazed at him dumbly for a few moments, then made a small, helpless gesture with her hands. 'I can't tell you the exact nature of the mission I was on,' she said, her voice barely audible. 'All I can say is that we – my colleagues and I – either had appalling bad luck, or else we were betrayed. There was an ambush . . . we never stood a chance.'

A deep frown creased her brow. 'The funny thing was, the Germans knew exactly who they wanted to take prisoner. They captured four of us. The other eight, they shot on the spot.'

Douglas saw that she was trying hard to stop tears bursting forth. Gently, he asked: 'Did they hurt you much?'

She shook her head. 'Knocked me about a little, but nothing serious . . . They planned to torture the others first, in the hope that I would break. God knows what they're doing to them now.' Her eyes were tortured.

'Then they brought you in,' she went on. 'God only knows how they knew about us. Their intelligence never used to be as good as that. I suppose they were going to play us off one against the other.'

Terrible pictures were flitting across Douglas's mind. He forced them out. He was certain, deep down, that if they had tortured Colette, he would have talked.

He leaned back against the wall and gave a deep sigh.

'What a bloody awful mess! We walked straight into this one, and no mistake.'

Making an enormous effort, he pulled himself together. 'All right. We can't help what's already happened. There's still time to do what we came to do. As far as I am concerned, the mission is definitely on.'

'May I ask what your mission is?' Colette said quietly. 'I may be able to help in some way.' Douglas raised an inquiring eyebrow at Fitzroy, who nodded.

'We came here to kill Rommel,' Douglas told her. She stared at him, her eyes wide. Then she said:

'You're going to have to hurry. I happen to know that he leaves for Germany tomorrow morning.'

Thirty miles north-west of Evreux – for that was where Douglas and his party were in hiding – the subject of their conversation was shaving, standing stripped to the waist in front of the mirror. He was pleased with his reflection; weeks of touring the coastal fortifications had given him a deep tan. Lucie would like that.

He scraped the razor carefully round his square, set jawline. He hummed as he shaved. Tomorrow, on his way home, he would stop off in Paris and do some shopping; some perfume for Lucie, and maybe a few other odds and ends too, and something for his son, Manfred.

It was time he got to know Manfred, he told himself. He had hardly seen the boy these last few years. And now Manfred, at the age of only fifteen, had just enlisted in the *Luftwaffe* anti-aircraft auxiliaries. It was a big step for the lad, the start of a whole new life. He was glad that Manfred had arranged a few days' leave, to coincide with his own; they could go shooting or rabbiting together in the woods, and catch up on lost time.

A sudden pounding on the bathroom door almost made Rommel nick himself. He swore, then bellowed: 'Yes! What is it?'

The door opened, and Rommel's operations officer, Colonel Tempelhoff, stepped into the luxurious tiled room. Rommel looked at him in surprise.

'You're up early, Hans-Georg,' he said. 'What's the matter?'

Tempelhoff's face was troubled. 'It's about that British officer who was picked up when the RAF 'plane crashed near Evreux the night before last, *Herr Feldmarschall*,' he said, then paused.

'Well, go on, man,' Rommel said impatiently. 'Has he recovered consciousness? Is he here?'

Tempelhoff looked embarrassed. 'That's just it, sir. He's escaped.'

'What!' Rommel threw down his razor, his face red with sudden rage. 'How?'

'Well, it seems that *Stürmbannführer* von Radusch decided to interrogate him personally –'

'Damn that man!' Rommel roared. 'My orders were that the British officer was to be brought here immediately. I'll have Radusch's innards!'

'Von Radusch is dead, sir,' Tempelhoff said bluntly. 'Someone helped the British officer to escape, and killed Radusch in the process. With a crossbow bolt in the back of the head.'

'A crossbow bolt! Damn. Damn, DAMN!' Rommel took a kick at the waste bucket that stood under the washbasin and sent it flying across the room. It hit the wall, cracking a tile.

He grabbed a towel and rubbed shaving foam from his face. He was breathing hard, but appeared to have regained control of himself.

'Do we know who was behind this?' he asked. 'The Resistance?'

Tempelhoff shook his head. 'We have yet to establish that, *Herr Feldmarschall*. The captured British officer is a Commando, and there must have been others on the aircraft. The British would not use a large 'plane for just one man. I have spoken to the *Abwehr*' – he named the German military intelligence service – 'and they believe, as I do, that the British have infiltrated a team of Commandos to carry out some special mission, possibly sabotage.'

Rommel gazed at his reflection in the mirror. His penetrating grey-blue eyes stared back.

'Or assassination,' he said softly. 'I wonder. I wouldn't put it past Montgomery.'

'Sir?' Tempelhoff looked at him questioningly. Rommel slapped his palm against the rim of the washbasin.

'Tempelhoff,' he said, 'if you were the British, and you wished to cause the maximum disruption to our defences just prior to an invasion, how would you go about it?'

Tempelhoff frowned. 'Well, sir,' he said after a few moments of thought, 'I would try to destroy our ammunition and fuel supplies – cut communications, and that sort of thing.'

Rommel waved a hand in the air. 'Bah! The Allied forces are doing all that as it is. It would take thousands of Commandos to improve on what the bombers are already doing. What else? Suppose only a handful of Commandos were involved?'

'In that case, sir, I would endeavour to eliminate key personnel. Such as –'

He stopped in mid-sentence and stared at Rommel, his mouth suddenly agape. Rommel grinned. 'Yes, that's right, Tempelhoff. Such as me. *Especially* me. So,' he said thoughtfully, 'there is a team of English assassins, number unknown, at large in the countryside, probably getting ready to kill me, doubtless with the aid of the French Resistance.'

'That's another thing, sir,' Tempelhoff said. 'A woman – a British agent, we think – also escaped from Evreux asylum at the same time as the Commando officer. Radusch said over the telephone that he had quite a file on her. I haven't seen it.'

'Well, see if you can get hold of it,' Rommel instructed. 'It might give us some clue as to what this is all about. You can telephone me at Herrlingen if there are any unusual developments.' He laughed suddenly. 'If I am the English Commandos' target, I am going to prove a very elusive one!'

'You are still going ahead with your leave, sir?'

Rommel looked at him in surprise. 'But of course, Hans-Georg! There will be no invasion before the twentieth of June. Have you forgotten about those other Commandos, captured a while ago? The ones who landed in the Somme estuary?'

There had been two officers and three men. The officers had been interviewed personally by Rommel, having been blindfolded and brought to his chateau. In the course of this interview, they had let slip that an invasion was coming, but they had hinted that it would not take place for some time – which appeared to confirm Rommel's own suspicions.

What Rommel did not know was that the Commandos had been deliberately planted by British Intelligence. At the expense of their own liberty, they had been sent to feed misleading information to the German High Command.

Whether they had succeeded or not was something British Intelligence had yet to establish. For this purpose, a French Resistance cell had been briefed to keep a close watch on Rommel's Headquarters, and to radio back to England every detail of how Rommel's staff reacted. If business carried on as usual, with no special flurry of activity, it would mean that the Germans had fallen for the Commandos' story. The Resistance had reliable contacts inside the chateau.

But something had gone badly wrong. The Resistance cell had been ambushed, and some of its members were reported to have been captured. The need to know their fate, and Rommel's intentions, was imperative.

Which was why Major Walter Fitzroy had been sent to France at the last moment – together with an SAS team whose mission now seemed impossible.

In the storeroom in Evreux, Douglas gazed at Colette with incredulity.

'How on earth can you know that?' he asked.

'Suffice to say that I do know it, Callum. I only wish that I was in a position to let our people in England know, too.'

Fitzroy came over and sat beside Douglas so that he could speak without being overheard by Marc, who was still busily forking hay from the cart.

'Very well,' he said, 'I might as well tell you what I know.' Briefly, he recounted the story of the captured Commandos.

'It's all a big bluff to deceive Rommel, d'you see? If he really is going off on leave, it means that it has worked.'

'So why the hell are we here?' Douglas asked angrily. Fitzroy coughed, as though covering up embarrassment.

'To put it bluntly, you're a sort of insurance policy,' he said. 'Until now, you see, we had no idea whether Rommel had swallowed our story or not. Well, it seems that he has, and is going to spend a couple of merry weeks at home. So he'll be well off the scene when things begin to happen.'

He looked at Douglas over the top of his glasses. 'However, if things had turned out differently, your job would have been to go in and knock him off. Luckily, you can forget all about that now.'

Douglas rose and stood with his legs apart. His head had suddenly ceased to hurt, and rising anger had made his mind perfectly clear. Liam Conolly smiled with inward satisfaction when Douglas spoke; the Boss was his old self again.

Douglas stared down at Fitzroy. 'The more I hear of this, the less I like it,' he said. 'The Germans are on to us, there can be no doubt about that. It can't be just coincidence that they were waiting for us at the landing ground.'

The SAS officer's face was very grim. 'This operation has already cost the lives of two RAF men. We owe them something. We came here to kill Rommel, and that is precisely what we are going to do.'

CHAPTER SIX

There was a sudden pounding on the door. Marc, who had just finished unloading the hay, indicated that Douglas and the others were to get out of sight behind a pile of sacks, then he crossed the room and opened the door a fraction. Douglas heard him carry on a hurried conversation, then he closed the door again and came over to speak to Fitzroy, who translated.

'The Germans are bringing reinforcements into Evreux,' he said. 'They've already begun house-to-house searches in the area around the asylum, and they are arresting people on the streets. I can't risk going back to the farm now, at least not with the horse and cart. Marc has come up with a pretty good idea, though. If we use his horses, we can take a short cut. There's a bridle-path just up the road, apparently, and it will take us into the open country in just a few minutes. There'll be plenty of cover in the woods. But we must move quickly, before the search reaches this part of the town.'

He grinned at Douglas. 'Marc is bringing you some clothing, Callum. You look a bit conspicuous as it is. That bandage had better come off, too.'

'I'll see to it,' Colette said. The sight of Douglas's scalp wound made her grimace.

'It looks messy,' she said, 'but it's not very deep. I'll take a proper look at it when we get to the farm. Meanwhile, I'll just put a pad on it.'

She fashioned a pad from a strip of bandage and placed it carefully on the cut. A beret, brought by Marc with a bundle of other clothing, held the improvised dressing in place.

Marc told Fitzroy that he would have one of his men drive the horse and cart back to the farm later. He had already given instructions for six of his own horses to be saddled up, and had posted a man at the end of the narrow street as a lookout.

Soon afterwards, the sound of hooves told them that the animals were being brought out into the yard. Marc opened the storeroom door again, peered out and then beckoned to the others to follow him.

Douglas tucked the dead ss officer's Luger into a pocket of the baggy jacket Marc had brought him. Sansom had already taken his lightweight crossbow to pieces, which he stowed away about his person. Apart from the Commando knife carried by Conolly, these were the only weapons they possessed, although Douglas learned to his relief that the MP-40s and their ammunition – including his own – had all been retrieved from the aircraft and were with the remainder of his party at the farm where they had taken refuge.

They mounted up on the magnificent horses, graceful Arabian creatures, and set off down the narrow street in single file. The man at the far end signalled that the coast was clear and they moved past him at the walk, turning left into the main road. It was cobbled, and a high wall flanked each side, providing welcome cover. After a quarter of a mile the wall gave way to railings on the right-hand side, enclosing what appeared to be a school with a small chapel standing nearby. The bridle-path Marc had mentioned ran between the two buildings; it was a sunken lane, with gorse bushes dotted along its banks.

The long, straight lane went on for a long way, ending in a field where dairy cattle were grazing. Marc bent down from the saddle to open a gate, closing it after the others had passed through.

The cows looked up for a moment, startled, as the cavalcade went by, then returned to their grazing. The riders crossed the open ground, looking round them watchfully as they did so, but there was no one else in sight.

Fitzroy came up to ride side-by-side with Douglas. 'I've got my bearings now,' he said. He pointed across the rolling countryside. 'The farm is over there, to the south-west. Marc is taking us in a big semi-circle around Evreux. Most of the route runs through woodland, as I said earlier, but there's one bit of open ground where we shall have to be particularly careful, because it crosses the approach to Evreux aerodrome. It's about five miles, all told.'

'What time is it now?' Douglas asked. His watch had been taken from him by the Germans, along with everything else.

'Just gone seven o'clock,' the other replied. He looked sideways at Douglas.

'I know what you're thinking,' he said quietly.

'I'm thinking whether we are going to have enough time to get across country after we have joined the others and nail Rommel before he goes home,' Douglas said. 'I reckon we have twenty-four hours from now, at the very outside. Look, you know a lot about the man. How does he normally travel – by special train, or car?'

'Car, usually,' Fitzroy told him. 'He likes to make un-scheduled calls on people as he goes.'

'He must lead a charmed life,' Douglas said. 'I'm surprised the Resistance hasn't had a go at him already.'

Colette, who was riding close behind them and who had overheard their conversation, chipped in.

'The main reason is that the brief of the Resistance in this part of France is to gather intelligence and, when the time comes, to disrupt communications,' she said. 'They have no orders to carry out assassinations. Besides, Rommel is very popular. He has made friends with many of the local farmers – shoots on their land, borrows ferrets from them to go rabbiting, and that sort of thing. Or so they say,' she added.

Douglas looked round at her and smiled. Apart from the small caress in the hay cart, no sign of affection had passed between them. There was no room for outward signs of emotion in their present situation, but they were both fighting an inward battle with their feelings, and each knew it.

Douglas thought for a moment, then said: 'We'll take a look at a map when we reach the farm, and plan our course of action then. You don't have to come with us, Walter. I suggest you lie low at the farm and let the war come to you. The invasion won't be long now.'

'That's all very well, old son, but my job isn't over,' Fitzroy said. 'I've got to find a radio and let London know that Rommel has swallowed our bait. All right – I've come round to your way of thinking. If we can kill him, so much the better. But there's no chance of an assault on his HQ now, is there?'

Douglas shook his head. 'Hardly. There isn't time. Our best bet will be to lay an ambush along the road somewhere.'

They were moving through woodland now, the horses trotting along well-beaten paths. From time to time they crossed tracts of open meadowland that lay between the wooded areas, and twice they passed the ruins of what must once have been magnificent houses, mediaeval mansions destroyed in the interminable wars of centuries past, or perhaps in the Revolution itself.

At the edge of one open stretch, Marc reined in and held up his hand. The riders paused on the edge of the trees.

'The perimeter of Evreux airfield is about a mile and a half away, over on the left,' Fitzroy warned. 'There's a flak tower over there. Look – you can just see the top of it, above the trees.'

Douglas looked, and saw what Fitzroy meant. A tall, circular structure stood among the woods several hundred yards away. Douglas made out a four-barrelled anti-aircraft gun, situated on top of it.

His eyes travelled from the flak tower to the valley that separated the two stretches of woodland on their route, and back again.

'By my reckoning, we'll be visible from that tower for about two hundred yards as we cross the valley,' he commented. 'We'd better go across slowly, and in single file, and do our best to make it look as though we're out for a morning ride. Let's hope the gunners haven't woken up yet.'

They moved off at the walk. In the valley the sunlight was strong and the night's dew had evaporated from the tall grasses, which bent and then sprang upright again as the horses passed.

In the top of the flak tower, a bored *Luftwaffe* NCO, eager for his shift to come to an end in an hour's time, picked up his binoculars and looked at the distant riders. He frowned. Lone horsemen, or perhaps horsemen in pairs, were a frequent enough sight in the valley; they were usually German officers in smart riding dress, and they were sometimes accompanied by very attractive women. But it was unusual to see six riders at the same time, and there was something distinctly odd about this lot. It was difficult to tell at this distance, even with the aid of his binoculars, but they seemed to be peasants; at any rate they were wearing rough clothing, except for the man who led the file. As far as the NCO could see, he was wearing proper riding boots and breeches.

The flak gunner was a good NCO. He had served on the eastern front, where partisans were troublesome, and had learned the hard way to keep his wits about him. Those riders seemed distinctly suspicious. It wasn't anything he could pin down – just a kind of sixth sense in the misery of the Russian front.

He had no wish to go back there, and that was another reason for reporting what he had seen. If he failed to do so, and something happened . . .

He lifted the handset of a field telephone and twirled the handle. A mile or so away, the lieutenant on duty in the command post that controlled the flak batteries ringing Evreux answered his call. The officer was less than polite.

'You are supposed to be watching the sky, not the scenery,' he snapped. 'In any case, what is so significant about half a dozen people out riding?'

The NCO explained as best he could. The lieutenant snorted down the mouthpiece. 'A hunch! Don't be ridiculous. What? You want your report placed in the log? Don't be impertinent!'

He slammed down the receiver. Nevertheless, he did record the NCO's call; it was procedure, and quite an automatic action.

When the lieutenant's relief arrived fifty minutes later, the first thing he did was to scan the log to see if there had been any special occurrences before he initialled it, so completing the handover.

'It's been a quiet night,' he said. Too quiet, he thought. No big formations of night bombers had passed overhead for nearly a week. The Tommies were certainly up to something.

His finger ran down the page until it reached the most recent entry, and stopped. 'What's this?' he asked.

'Oh, it's that idiot Haas, in number five position. His years on the Russian front must have addled his brain. He saw half a dozen riders crossing the valley an hour or so ago and is imagining all sorts. Thinks they could be something to do with the Resistance.'

The other officer gazed at him. 'Don't you know about the alert?' he asked incredulously.

'What alert? What are you talking about?'

'That fellow they picked up the night before last, wandering around near that Tommy 'plane. The one that crashed near Conches. Well, it turns out that he was some sort of British Commando. They brought him to the asylum in Evreux and were just going to interrogate him, along with some Resistance people they had captured, when he escaped. Or rather, he was helped to escape. An ss officer was murdered. One of the terrorists – a woman, by all accounts – got away too. It all happened at about four thirty this morning. Everybody has been warned to look out for them.'

'Oh, my God! A woman, you said.' The nco in the flak tower had said something about one of the riders having long hair.

An hour had gone by since then, and he had chosen to do nothing.

Frantically, he made a grab for the telephone; but his colleague, who had never liked him very much anyway, had already beaten him to it.

Douglas was feeling desperately tired, but he knew that the chance to sleep was a long way off. The enemy's search would soon extend to the countryside around Evreux; he and his team had to get away quickly, and that meant travelling across country in broad daylight.

He looked at the others, seated around the big farmhouse table. With Colette and Fitzroy, there were ten in all; too many to travel as one party, especially on horseback.

Marc, after some persuasion, had agreed to let them use his precious horses. The farmer had managed to acquire four more. Douglas, sticking his neck out, had promised that both men would be more than adequately compensated by the British government when France was liberated. He would, he had told them, do his best to ensure that the animals came to no harm.

They had breakfasted on bread and cheese and fresh milk, and the farmer's wife had provided them with some small, round cheeses for their journey. Both she and the farmer were showing signs of agitation.

'They want us to leave,' Fitzroy said, 'and I can't say I blame them. They've done more than enough for us already. It would be a tragedy if anything were to happen to them, with the invasion so close.'

Douglas nodded. 'I agree. We'll get cracking. We're going to have to split up, though, and rendezvous at various points en route. I've marked them on the map, so pass it round and make a note. As you will see, we are heading for a spot close to the Rouen-Paris road, just to the west of Mantes. Rommel will have to pass that way tomorrow morning, and with any luck we'll be waiting for him.'

He divided his team into four groups, ensuring that as far as possible there was someone who spoke French with each group. Colette was to travel with Barber and the dependable Brough, Fitzroy with Olds and Lambert. Conolly, who knew some French, was to go with Sansom, while Douglas himself was to travel with Mitchell. The French language was by no means one of Douglas's accomplishments, although he knew enough to struggle by.

Fitzroy was worried about getting his radio message to London, and said so. The radio equipment carried by

Mitchell could be used to make contact with special duties aircraft or ships offshore, but it did not have sufficient range to reach England.

It was Colette who supplied a possible solution. She explained about the RAF's special 'Ascension' aircraft, which circled high over the Channel every night at set times to make contact with Resistance groups. Fitzroy agreed to give her idea a try.

A few minutes later, they said their farewells to the farmer and his wife, and to Marc. Quietly, Douglas drew Brough to one side.

'Look after her, Stan,' he said. 'I'm sending Colette with you because I want her to come through this in one piece. She's as tough as nails, but I don't know how much more she can take. If anyone can see her through, it's you.'

Brough was touched by the trust his officer placed in him. 'Don't worry, sir. She'll be all right. Barber's a good sort, too.'

'Thanks, Stan. Well, we'd better be on our way. Remember, keep to the woods as much as you can. And good luck to you all.'

He said his own brief goodbye to Colette and then mounted up, patting his horse's neck as he watched the other groups leave the farm and trot away towards the woods to the east, following different paths that gradually caused them to diverge.

'Come on, Mitch,' he said. 'It's going to be a long, hot day.'

He was wrong. Half an hour later, as they plodded on across country, a breeze sprang up. It rose to wind strength within minutes, or so it seemed, and in its wake, scudding across the land from the south-west, came dark clouds.

It rained. The water came down in sheets, dancing from the tree branches in clouds of spray, soaking the riders and their mounts. It made Douglas want to shout out loud. He welcomed it with all his heart. It formed a protective cocoon around them, sheltering them from enemy eyes. It made him feel alive again.

On the other side of the English Channel, a very large number of men felt anything but alive. Some of them had been aboard their landing ships since the first day of June. At first, their lives had been bearable, but now, with a Force Five wind from the south-west churning the water into grey and white chaos, it was a different tale.

It was bad enough for the many thousands on the decks of the ships, sick and cold as they were, but for the thousands huddled below decks in the constant stench of vomit, it was torment. To be hurled ashore on the alien beaches, in the face of murderous gunfire and a host of other unknown perils, would be infinitely preferable to this agony. The men had lost all interest in everything; even the sight of the great, grey warships that prowled among the anchored convoys, soon to fling their massive shells on to a hundred points along the enemy coast, failed to excite comment.

The worst affected prayed for death, or at least for the landings to come soon. For many of them, it would amount to the same thing.

The rain began to ease a little by noon, when Douglas and his men made their first rendezvous, in a small wood overlooking the river Eure. They were all sodden, but their journey had been without incident, thanks mainly to the rain.

In the distance, from their vantage point, they could see a small town astride the river. They identified it as Pacy-sur-Eure. Douglas was pleased with their progress; they had come a little less than half-way towards their ultimate objective. He was less pleased with the terrain that lay ahead of them. It was mostly open country, and to complicate matters even further there seemed to be nowhere they could cross the river under cover. A road ran along the opposite bank.

'We could leave the horses and continue on foot,' Conolly suggested. 'We've got about fifteen miles still to go. We could manage that easily by dark.'

Douglas shook his head. 'No. We need the horses. If we run into trouble, we wouldn't stand a chance on foot. Besides, the river looks to be pretty swollen, and there aren't any bridges. We'll have to swim for it, and it makes sense to let the horses do the work. Liam, give me your binoculars, will you?'

Conolly handed the glasses to him. Douglas focused on a spot on the far side of the river.

'There's another one of those ruined buildings over there, just by that clump of trees,' he said. 'We'll cross the river singly, then take cover in the ruins until everyone is safely across. I'll go first.'

He made his way down the slope, letting the horse pick its own way. At the water's edge he dismounted and, clinging to the saddle, urged the animal forward. It entered the water reluctantly, stumbling a little, then kicked itself into the current with a splash that almost dislodged Douglas.

The horse crabbed its way through the fast-flowing water, drifting a little downstream, Douglas clung on tightly, floating by the animal's side. He felt the horse's hooves make contact with the river bed and seized the reins, finding his own footing.

He held the horse motionless on the river bank for a few moments, checking his pack and MP-40, which were slung across the animal's back in front of the saddle, and surveying the adjacent road. There was no one in sight, and no sign of danger, so he mounted up again and urged the horse towards the ruins on the hillside beyond.

The broken walls stood grey and silent. Douglas approached to within a few yards, then slid from the saddle and unshipped his MP-40. He cocked it, leaving the safety catch on, and led the horse towards a gap in the wall, negotiating fallen masonry. Swallows, braving the rain, twittered around holes high up in the stonework. It was all very peaceful. The scene, as he went through the gap, reminded him of an English abbey; there were tall arched windows in a large fragment of wall on the other side of a grassy square.

Something cold and hard jabbed into the side of his neck. '*Doucement*,' said a soft and sinister voice. '*Donnez-moi votre carabine.*'

Douglas knew enough French to understand that command. Wordlessly, looking straight ahead, he handed the weapon over. His other hand still clutched the horse's reins.

'*Bon. En avant, mais très lentement.*'

He obeyed, walking forward slowly until he and the horse were standing in the shelter of the ruins. He saw at once that he was surrounded by men, a dozen of them, creeping out from niches in the walls and from behind the stone pillars that had once supported the roof.

They wore a kind of uniform: roll-neck jumpers, leather jerkins, riding breeches and leggings. Some were bare-headed, others sported the traditional beret. They carried an assortment of weapons, ranging from shotguns to Sten sub-machine-guns, all of which were pointing at Douglas. He knew at once that he could only be in the hands of the Resistance.

'*Il y a des autres*!' hissed one of the men, who had been keeping a lookout through the gap in the wall. The man with the gun at Douglas's neck pushed him, still leading the horse, deeper inside the ruins, out of sight of whoever was coming up the slope. Douglas could not see who it was.

The next rider received the treatment that Douglas had just experienced. The SAS officer, who had been forced to stand with his face to the wall, could only wait helplessly for what might happen next. He cursed himself bitterly for having allowed himself to be taken by surprise. His captors might be friendly; on the other hand, they might not. They looked a pretty hard-bitten crew.

Suddenly, one of the men gave an exclamation, followed by what sounded like a delighted cry. A moment or two later, the muzzle of the Sten was removed from Douglas's neck. Behind him, everyone was talking at once. Cautiously, he turned round.

A huge Frenchman had Colette in a bear hug and was waltzing clumsily around with her, oblivious to her soaked condition. The rest were standing around them in a circle, laughing. Douglas seemed to have been completely forgotten.

Suddenly, there was a silence as a man of medium build emerged from the shadows. He wore more or less the same clothing as the others, but had no headgear. His hair was fair and curly, as was his beard.

The circle of men made way for him respectfully. He went up to Colette, took her by the hand and addressed her in perfect English.

'We are very, very happy to see you,' he said. 'We heard that you had been captured, and feared the worst.'

Before she could reply, Douglas gave a loud cough. The fair-haired man turned towards him, smiling. He came up and extended his hand.

'My apologies for the reception committee,' he said. 'We can't be too careful, as you will appreciate.'

'That's quite all right,' Douglas said politely. 'There's just one thing, though – I have eight more men out there somewhere, and if I don't give them the all-clear signal very soon, they are going to come in here shooting.'

The other man waved towards the gap in the wall. 'By all means. We want to avoid any accidents.'

Douglas went over to the gap and looked out. A horse was standing some distance away, tethered loosely to a bush, but there was no sign of its rider.

'It's okay,' Douglas called. 'You can come in. There's no danger.'

Brough appeared from behind some rocks, his MP-40 at the ready. 'Are you sure, sir?' he asked.

'Quite sure, Stan. Come and join the party.'

Brough led his horse into the ruins, followed by the others at intervals of a few minutes. Conolly brought up the rear and looked at the gathering in some amazement. He looked distinctly uncomfortable when the big Frenchman grabbed him and kissed him on both cheeks.

Colette laughed and introduced the officers to the fair-haired man, explaining that he was known as Olivier. It was obviously not his real name.

'You speak very good English,' Douglas said. The other laughed.

'That's hardly surprising, old boy. I *am* English,' he explained. 'I'm here to give these chaps a hand. I specialize in demolition, you see.'

It was Colette's turn to laugh. 'Olivier is the chap who

created some havoc with a German mechanised infantry division last winter,' she said. 'You may remember – it was just after our episode in the Camargue. The division was on its way to counter the landings at Anzio, and he sealed it neatly inside a tunnel in the Alps.'

'Yes, I do remember,' Douglas said. 'A very fine effort, if I may say so.'

Olivier assumed a modest expression. 'Oh, I don't know. I've always had a certain talent for that sort of thing. I used to put chewing gum on my young brother's model railway track and derail his engines, so I suppose I got off to a flying start.'

'What are you doing here?' Douglas asked.

'Blowing up railway lines,' Olivier told him. 'It's a bit tame, but it all helps.'

'It's not so tame when you get ambushed,' Colette said quietly. Douglas saw anguish touch her face briefly.

'Ah, yes,' said Olivier, 'I'm sorry, it was just a thoughtless comment.' He turned back to Douglas. 'You are here for a specific purpose, I presume?'

Douglas told him what it was, and Olivier stroked his beard thoughtfully.

'That's quite an enterprise,' he said. 'I wonder if we can help. Where are you going to do it?'

Douglas took out his map and showed him the spot, where the road to Mantes ran close to the Seine.

Olivier inspected it for a minute, then said: 'I know that stretch, and I have an idea. Rommel will most certainly be travelling with a strong escort, and the kind of ambush you have in mind will be very risky, and probably unsuccessful. I think we should try to bring down the roof on his head, so to speak.'

'We?' queried the SAS officer. Olivier smiled, his eyes twinkling.

'Oh, yes. I don't want to miss this one. Look, here's what I mean.'

He touched the map. 'Just here, on the south side of the road, there is a rocky overhang. Well, it's not exactly an overhang, but near enough. Now, a few carefully planted explosive charges should be enough to bring a fair old tonnage of rock tumbling down just as Rommel's little convoy is passing that very spot. It should create some splendid confusion, don't you think?'

Douglas pondered the idea for a few moments, then said: 'I think it's first class. Barber, over there, is our explosives man; perhaps you can concoct something with him. The question is, can we do it in time? I mean, there isn't much darkness to cover us while we lay the charges.'

Olivier looked up at the lowering clouds. 'In my opinion, it will be dark early tonight. But in any case, the preparations will only take a couple of hours. We have the rest of the day to get into position. Perhaps we can take turns at riding those wonderful horses. The ones who aren't riding can trot alongside. You can cover a lot of ground that way, hanging on to a stirrup.'

Douglas frowned. 'Travelling in a large group worries me,' he said. 'You've got a dozen men, and I have almost as many. Better if we split up, which was my original scheme, and rendezvous in the target area. Then we can make the final approach on foot.'

'Good idea,' Olivier said. 'Let's work out the details.' They shook hands on it.

CHAPTER SEVEN

In the chateau that served as his headquarters, Erwin Rommel, in dressing-gown and slippers, paced painfully up and down his study, hands clasped behind his back.

'Damn this rain!' he muttered. 'It makes my lumbago even worse.'

One of the three men who sat at the study table smiled. 'They say that the only cure for lumbago is churchyard mould, *Herr Feldmarschall*,' he quipped. The remark brought a glare from Rommel.

'I don't think that's funny, Speidel. And in future, when I summon you for a meeting, kindly present yourself at once.'

At first, Rommel had got on well with General Hans Speidel, who had been his chief of staff since April. Speidel was a fellow Swabian, in his mid-forties – a few years younger than Rommel – and, despite his bespectacled, intellectual air, had come with the highest recommendations, having served with distinction on the Russian front. Now a few irritations were beginning to creep into their working relationship; the least of them was Speidel's habit of playing Beethoven at full blast on his gramophone, the greatest a growing tendency to turn up for meetings at his convenience, and not the field marshal's.

Speidel would be in command of the coastal defences during Rommel's absence, and the purpose of this meeting was to go through any final details. On one point, Rommel was determined.

'Despite what General Geyr thinks,' he said, 'I am convinced that an Allied landing in Normandy will be a feint. The real invasion will take place across the Pas de Calais, and we need more armour in that area.'

He turned to the man who was sitting next to Speidel. He was a general, and wore the black uniform of the tanks.

'Mercke, how soon can you move the 112th Panzer Division north?' The 112th, which had been badly mauled in Russia, had been withdrawn to rest and refit. Now, up to full strength and equipped with the latest Tiger tanks, it had been assigned to the Western Front and was encamped near Chartres.

General Friedrich Mercke, the divisional commander, pursed his lips. 'We can begin the move immediately, *Herr Feldmarschall*,' he told Rommel, 'but we are short of fuel and ammunition. What I am saying is that once we are assigned to a new sector, we shall have to stay there. Assuming that the logistics situation does not change, we shall simply not have enough fuel to embark on any wild goose chases across France.'

Rommel nodded. He liked Mercke's forthright manner of speaking. He glanced briefly at Colonel Tempelhoff, the third man in the room, who was busily taking notes. Tempelhoff was recording every word of what was said in the room; Rommel did not want any subsequent 'misinterpretations' of his wishes.

'Very well. Are you in full agreement, Speidel?'

The latter inclined his head, giving his assent. Speidel did not like General Geyr, who was openly contemptuous of his abilities. Geyr had once been heard to say that although Speidel might have shone as a staff officer, he had never actually commanded anything bigger than an infantry company. The remark was true, and therefore it rankled all the more.

Rommel was visibly pleased. 'Good! I will arrange for the necessary movement orders to be drafted tonight. As you know, I am going to leave in the morning, Mercke. Perhaps you would care to travel part of the distance with me, after breakfast? From here, it is almost as easy to reach Chartres from Paris as to travel by Dreux. The roads are certainly better. You can take the movement order with you.'

Mercke offered his thanks, and Rommel rubbed his hands together. 'Then that just about wraps it up, gentlemen. There are just a few minor points I wish to discuss, then we shall retire to bed. And let us hope,' he concluded, rubbing his back again, 'that we awaken to sunshine!'

A few hundred feet above the tree-tops, ragged shreds of stratus cloud chased one another across the darkened sky, depositing a thin drizzle on the land below.

In the blackness among the trees that bordered the road twenty-one men and one woman crouched, cold and miserably wet, huddled against the tree trunks for shelter. From time to time, vehicles with masked headlights passed along the road, and on those occasions the people among the trees stirred and brought their weapons to the ready, in case the vehicles stopped and disgorged enemy troops.

Douglas stood up, shivering slightly. His head was hurting badly and he felt sick. Like all the others he was very hungry – the cheese provided by the farmer's wife had long since gone – but he would not touch his rations. He had no idea how long they might have to last.

He had no real idea, either, how they were going to get away after their task was completed, even assuming that they escaped with their lives. He had formed a sketchy plan of sorts, which involved splitting up the group and heading for a rendezvous near the coast, somewhere they could lie low and wait for the invasion. One step at a time, he told himself. Every hour they managed to stay alive would be another milestone passed.

At least the horses that had served them so well were safe. They were secure in a field some miles back, their saddles removed. Despite his discomfort, he smiled to himself as he visualized the utter astonishment of some farmer as he discovered an unexpected addition to his stock early the next morning.

He went over to where Olivier and Barber were kneeling on the wet ground. Not daring to show a light, they were working by touch alone as they prepared their explosive charges.

'How's it going?' he asked. It was Olivier who answered.

'Nearly ready. Can you give us some cover while we set this up, just in case?'

Douglas moved away and held a council of war with his men. He told them that the explosive charges were about to be laid.

'We'll move down and take up position under cover by the roadside,' he said. 'We will be the first line of defence if anything goes wrong. If it does, the operation is blown anyway, so our task will be to cover Olivier and Barber while they get into the woods. They will be completely exposed while they set the charges.'

He peered around him in the darkness. 'Walter, are you there?'

Fitzroy came up and crouched alongside him. 'I want you and Colette to stay in the woods with the Resistance boys,' Douglas said. 'Explain to them what we're doing. Their job, if necessary, will be to give covering fire for us as we fall back after the job's done. I hope it won't come to that, but we've had an easy passage so far. Let's expect trouble, then it won't take us by surprise.'

Olivier came up, announcing that he and Barber were ready. Douglas told him to wait five minutes, allowing he and his men to get into position. They crept out of the woods, descended a steep slope and stretched themselves in the sodden undergrowth close to the road, with ten yards between each man. The rocky overhang stuck out like a great fist on their left, overshadowing the road.

Olivier, who had already made a swift survey of the overhang before darkness fell, had worked out exactly where to place the charges for maximum effect. A series of fissures extended upwards from the base of the rock, and tumbled boulders extending down the slope as far as the road told of frequent landslides in the past.

'The whole bloody lot would have come down by itself one day, in any case,' he whispered to Barber as they carefully placed the charges – six in all – in the fissures. 'We're just hurrying it up a bit, that's all. There, that's it – we can start paying out the wire, now.'

At that moment, Barber seized his arm. 'Hold on a minute,' he said. 'I can hear something.'

Olivier listened for a moment, then said: 'You're right. Sounds like a motor bike. Time to get under cover, I think.'

They scrambled down and took shelter among the fallen rocks. The noise of the two-stroke engine grew louder, and a dim headlight came into view along the road, coming from the direction of Mantes.

Douglas and the others had also heard and seen the motor cycle. They flattened themselves against the ground, keeping their heads well down.

The roar of the motor cycle's engine died to a throaty burble. Douglas could hear the swish of tyres on the wet road. The sound stopped directly opposite him, and above the idling engine he could hear voices.

'*Danke, Hans. Du hast mein Leben gerettet. Ich muss mein Harn lassen!*'

'*Also, mach' schnell.*' The other voice sounded testy.

Douglas heard footsteps on the road, then the sound of boots shuffling through the grass. There was silence for a moment, then a prolonged swishing sound, accompanied by a drawn-out sigh. After half a minute, Douglas heard the unseen feet retrace their steps through the grass and on to the road again.

'*Besser?*'

'*Ja, wirklich!*'

The motor cycle's engine roared again. Douglas listened to its fading note. Only when it was so faint as to be almost unheard did he lift his head.

'That was a bit too close for comfort,' Conolly said, from his position a few yards away. 'Jerry patrol. At least it's not likely that there'll be another one for a good while.'

'I hope not,' said a disgruntled voice which Douglas identified as Lambert's. 'The bugger pissed all over me!'

Douglas told them to stop talking. Something moved behind him and Olivier's voice called out softly, telling him that he was paying out the thin cable that was wired up to the explosives.

Douglas ordered his men to fall back into the trees. There was nothing they could do now but wait. He decided to take a snack from his rations, after all, and told the others to do the same. They shared some of what they had with the Frenchmen. If they were going to get killed, Douglas thought, it might as well be with something in their stomachs.

Erwin Rommel was going to be delayed. There was no helping it. It was simply that he had woken up quite unable to move. The effort of doing so, and the roar of pain that had accompanied it, had brought his valet running to his room in alarm.

'Damn it,' Rommel shouted, 'get the doctor! And ask General Mercke to come here!'

It would take a full two hours of strenuous massage to free Rommel's knotted muscles; he knew that from bitter experience. How he longed for the African heat! That was the only time in years when his lumbago had never troubled him. Damn Europe, with its miserable climate! And on top of it all, he had to face a drive of several hours. But nothing, *nothing*, was going to interfere with his leave!

Mercke arrived, enquiring solicitously if there was anything he might do.

'No, Mercke, there unfortunately isn't,' Rommel said, 'but thank you anyway. You had better be on your way. You have your orders?'

'Yes, *Herr Feldmarschall*.' He produced an unsealed envelope. 'They only need your signature.'

'Very well. Give them to me, and a pen.'

Rommel signed the orders authorizing the movement of the 112th Panzer Division with some difficulty, for he was lying flat on his face, and handed them back to Mercke. The latter replaced them in the envelope and returned them to his pocket, still unsealed.

'To be on the safe side, take my escort as well,' Rommel instructed. 'Send them back when you reach Paris. You can pick up another there. With a bit of luck I'll be fit to travel by then.'

Presenting his condolences, Mercke saluted and left the room. In the drive outside the chateau his staff car was waiting alongside Rommel's. Both were of identical make. The escort, comprising a dozen heavily-armed motor cyclists, was also drawn up, half in front and half behind the staff cars. Mercke told its commander what Rommel had said.

A few minutes later, the tank general and his escort were moving off down the long drive. Rommel's personal driver, Corporal Daniel, watched them go and sighed, wondering how long it would be before he could set off on the journey home. He, too, was looking forward to a spot of leave. He only hoped, for the sake of his boss's temper, that the sun would be shining in Germany.

The rain had stopped now, but the morning was grey and overcast. Douglas and his men had taken it in turns to snatch a little sleep – or try to, for their clothing was wet through. The dawn found them bleary eyed, dirty and unshaven.

By seven o'clock, Douglas was beginning to worry. Rommel, with his reputation for being an early riser, should be on his way by now. Traffic was starting to build up on the road, adding to his anxiety. He and the others took it in turns to keep Conolly's binoculars trained on the spot where, in the distance, the road curved out of sight, following the line of the Seine.

It was approaching seven thirty when Conolly, whose turn it was with the binoculars, raised the alarm. He handed the glasses to Fitzroy, who was beside him. He trained them on the distant stretch of road, which was visible between the trees.

'Could be,' he murmured. 'Could be . . . looks like a staff car, and there's a heavy escort.'

'All right,' Douglas snapped, 'stand by. You all know what to do.'

Olivier, kneeling behind a tree trunk, pulled up the handle of the plunger, ready to make the contact that would bring a mass of rock plummeting down on to the road. He raised a silent prayer that everything would work.

They waited as the distant vehicle and its escort drew closer. 'It's a Horch,' Fitzroy exclaimed. 'Rommel has a Horch. It's got to be him. No one else would have that big an escort.'

'Wait for it.' Douglas looked round at the mixture of SAS men and Resistance fighters. Their tiredness seemed to have slipped away and there was an air of eagerness about them. He had ordered Colette to stay well back among the trees, mainly because she was armed only with the Luger he had taken from the SS officer.

The leading motor cyclists were approaching the rocky overhang, the roar of their engines deafening. Everything depended on perfect timing. Douglas looked at Olivier, his heart racing. Was he leaving it too late?

Olivier's shoulders hunched slightly and he rammed the plunger down hard. In the split second that followed, Douglas was conscious that he was holding his breath.

Six reports, barely audible above the noise of the motor cycle engines and sounding ridiculously inadequate, merged into one. Puffs of smoke burst from the overhanging crag just as the leading cyclists drew abreast of it.

Douglas had expected the rock face to fall outwards as it sundered from the main outcrop. Instead, it began to slide, barely perceptibly at first, then gathering momentum as it plunged down the slope. With a fearsome crackling noise the rock wall began to come apart, flinging massive chunks of jagged stone into the roadway. Douglas heard a screech of brakes as the Horch disappeared from sight behind a cloud of swirling dust and stone fragments.

'Open fire!' Douglas yelled, at the top of his voice. His small band of SAS men burst out of the trees, firing their MP-40s in short bursts at the leading riders. The latter, two of whom had already been peppered by razor-sharp stone fragments and who were careering wildly across the road, had no time to react. Within seconds, all six had been cut down. Only one managed to rise to his knees in the roadway, but before he could fire back at his attackers a burst from Mitchell knocked him over.

Meanwhile, Olivier's Resistance men, accompanied by Fitzroy, who was brandishing a revolver, were disappearing into the dust, Douglas's men charged into the road and followed them, coughing as they breathed in the grit. Douglas leaped over a boulder, and disjointed images gradually pieced themselves together in front of him.

The Horch had hit a slab of rock and overturned. It lay on its side, diagonally across the road, its front end smashed in. Douglas ran round it and saw three men sprawling in the road. One tried to crawl away and a Resistance fighter put a burst of Sten bullets into him at point-blank range. It was apparent that the other two were already dead.

The rear half of the motor cycle escort lay in a hopeless tangle, the riders lying where Olivier's men had shot them down. Only one, it seemed, had retained control of his machine and turned it round in a bid to escape, but the big Frenchman had picked him off with a high-powered rifle. He lay some distance away, his motor cycle on top of him.

Slowly, the dust began to subside, drifting down to lie in a grey layer on the road and the bodies. The echoes of the gunfire died away. The whole swift, bloody action had lasted no more than two minutes.

An idea was beginning to take shape in Douglas's mind. He shouted to Brough, who came running up.

'Stan, get our boys together and have them check out the motor bikes. See how many are still working. Also, strip the smocks and helmets from the Jerries. Put 'em in a pile over there, by the roadside. As fast as you can!'

Brough turned away, shouting orders, and Douglas strode over to where Fitzroy was bending over one of the bodies by the staff car. He looked up as Douglas approached, his face a mask of disappointment.

'It's not Rommel,' he said quietly. 'I'm afraid there's been a cock-up.'

He held up an identification card, which he had taken from the body. 'This is General Mercke, commanding the 112th

Panzer Division,' he announced. 'I found this, too. It's important.'

He showed Douglas some papers which he had extracted from a buff envelope. He grimaced a little as he did so; there was blood on his fingers.

'What is it?' Douglas asked.

'Something that could make all the difference to the success of the invasion,' Fitzroy told him. 'It's an order, signed by Rommel himself, deploying the 112th Panzer Division from its present location near Chartres to the Pas de Calais sector.'

Fitzroy stood up and stared down at the dead man. 'The 112th has been one of our main worries,' he said. 'It's a fresh division, equipped with the latest tanks, and the Germans have been holding it in reserve to take part in a counter-offensive against any Allied beach-head in Normandy. The fact that it is being ordered to move north means that the enemy is anticipating a full-scale invasion in the Pas de Calais, over the shortest Channel route.'

He bent down and carefully replaced the document in the dead general's inside pocket. 'We've got to make sure they go on believing it, Callum. And, what is equally as important, once the 112th Panzer Division crosses the Seine, we've got to try and keep it there somehow.'

Douglas looked at him questioningly.

Fitzroy gave a tired smile and shrugged. 'I might as well tell you, because time is so short and you have a right to know. The full invasion will take place in Normandy. And it will come within the next forty-eight hours.'

Douglas's mind was working overtime. 'Do those orders say which route the armour will take?' he asked.

'There is only one bridge over the Seine west of Paris which is still standing and which is strong enough to support heavy tanks,' Fitzroy told him 'and that is at Mantes. The RAF and USAAF have knocked all the others down. It's the only route the division can possibly take, without making a big detour to the east.'

Douglas inclined his head towards the body at his feet.

'You're assuming that the orders will still reach the division?' he asked. Fitzroy nodded.

'Stake my life on it. I know the Germans. It'll be the first thing they do, when they come to clear up the mess here.'

'Which won't be very long. We've got to get moving.' He paused, then said quietly: 'Thanks for telling me about Normandy. I know you weren't supposed to. But it's going to make life a lot easier. I know where to head for, now.'

He looked around and saw Olivier, conferring with his men. Douglas went over to him and drew him to one side. 'We got the wrong man,' he said.

'I know,' Olivier said. 'Pity about that. Who did we get?'

Douglas told him. He also told him about the 112th Panzer Division's movement order. 'What are your plans now?' he asked.

Olivier grinned at him. 'Oh, I think blowing up a bridge at Mantes sounds like a good idea,' he said. 'Once the tanks are safely on the other side, of course.'

'Funny, I was thinking exactly the same thing,' Douglas grinned back. At that moment, Brough came up and reported that seven of the motor cycles were still serviceable. 'We've collected the camouflage smocks – some of 'em are a bit messy – and the helmets, too.'

'Tell the lads to start putting them on,' he said, 'but tell them to hang on to their civilian clothing too.'

He suddenly spotted Colette. She had come down from the wood and was sitting by the roadside. She looked pale and ill.

'Colette is going to have to put some German gear on too,' Douglas said. 'She doesn't look at all well. The sooner we get her away from this, the better. She can ride pillion with me.'

'Right, sir. I'll pick the five best bikes. They've all got full tanks, by the way.'

Douglas nodded, then turned back to Olivier. 'Well, thanks for everything,' he said. 'We couldn't have done this without your help. We may not have got Rommel, but we've come up with something that could be every bit as important.'

He held out his hand. 'Good luck in Mantes. Perhaps we'll meet up again, somewhere along the line.'

Olivier grasped the proffered hand firmly. 'I have no doubt of it,' he said.

'Good luck to you, as well – wherever it is you're heading.'

One of the Resistance men, who had been watching the road to the east, gave a sudden shout. Olivier slung his Sten gun over his shoulder.

'Enemy trucks approaching,' he said urgently. 'This lot will hold them up while we get away. The Jerries won't catch us in the woods.'

He ran off to round up his men. Conolly threw a camouflage smock at Douglas, who put it on. He also donned a steel helmet, and Conolly handed him a pair of goggles. 'We're all set, boss,' the Irishman said. 'Lead on.'

Douglas threw his leg over one of the motor cycles, a powerful BMW, and kicked it into life, blessing the excellence of German engines. Colette got on behind him and clung on to the pack that was strapped to his back.

Douglas gave a last look round, receiving a thumbs-up from each of the five riders and their passengers. He looked for Olivier, but the Resistance fighters had already melted away into the woods.

He opened the throttle and sent the BMW roaring along the road, with the others in close pursuit. The wind felt good against his face, sweeping some of the weariness from him.

A couple of miles from the scene of the ambush, the riders rounded a bend and came upon half a dozen German army lorries, travelling in the opposite direction. The motor cyclists were past them in moments; even if the soldiers in the trucks had noticed anything suspicious there was nothing they could have done.

Nevertheless, Douglas judged that it was time to get off the main road, and when a minor road appeared up ahead, apparently leading away to the south-west, he took it. After another couple of miles or so he brought the motor cycle to a halt so that he could get his bearings and, with the aid of his map, work out the best route to follow.

It was then that the fighter-bombers swept down upon them.

CHAPTER EIGHT

The two Hawker Typhoons had taken off from their base at Thorney Island, near Portsmouth, less than half an hour earlier on what the RAF called a 'Rhubarb' – a brief incursion into enemy-occupied France to shoot up whatever worthwhile targets they could find.

They had crossed the Channel under low cloud, keeping well clear of the gunners in the massive convoys that rode at anchor off the English coast, and had briefly pulled up into the clouds as they passed over the Bay of the Seine, to avoid the enemy flak. Then, dropping clear of the clouds again, they had headed inland, looking for the airfields at Evreux and St Andre.

Thwarted by the low cloud and drizzle, they had failed to find their objectives and so had turned north towards the Seine, hoping to find some enemy river traffic or, at least, a train or two on the adjacent railway lines. Instead, they had found a line of motor cyclists, heading across country at considerable pace. The young flying officer who was leading the Typhoons reasoned that they could only be Germans, and gave the order to attack. As he did so, he saw the cyclists come to a stop and group together. So much the better, he decided.

To gain maximum surprise, the two Typhoon pilots dropped down as low as they dared and placed a low hill between themselves and the group of cyclists. They swooped around the far slope of the hill, wingtips almost brushing the trees, and bore down on the group of men, their reflector sights on.

It was only then that Douglas and the others saw and heard the howling aircraft.

Mitchell saw them first, and screamed a warning. Douglas, acting automatically, seized Colette and bodily hurled her into a ditch by the side of the road, shielding her with his own body.

The four cannon of the leading Typhoon barked, their sound clearly audible above the thunder of its engine. Explosive shells sent up fountains of dirt from the road.

The second aircraft came in, its guns also pounding. There were more staccato explosions. Shrapnel ripped through the hedge above Douglas, showering him with leaves and twigs.

The Typhoons pulled up into the low cloud. The snarl of their engines died away. Cautiously, Douglas raised his head, then rolled clear of Colette and raised himself on one knee.

Someone was lying in the middle of the road in a spreading pool of blood. Douglas scrambled over to him. It was Fitzroy, and Douglas saw at once that his left arm was shattered.

Fitzroy looked up at him dreamily. His glasses had fallen off, and his eyes were unfocussed. 'What a bloody silly thing to happen,' he whispered. 'Never mind – I think I can get up now.'

'Lie still,' Douglas said firmly, placing a hand on the intelligence officer's chest. 'Liam, give me a hand, will you?'

Together, they cut away the sleeve of Fitzroy's camouflage smock and the material of the peasant's jacket beneath. Douglas winced at what he saw. The arm was riddled with shell fragments and broken in at least three places.

Colette knelt beside the injured man and applied a tourniquet beneath the shoulder, stemming the flow of blood. Keeping the arm immobile with improvised splints, fashioned from straight pieces of wood from the hedgerow, they bandaged it with field dressings. Douglas gave Fitzroy a morphine tablet and a drink of water. Fitzroy looked up at him gratefully.

'Thanks, Callum. Help me to sit up, will you?'

91

Douglas carefully placed an arm behind Fitzroy's back and brought him slowly up to a sitting position. He moaned.

'Christ, it hurts! Sorry, never did have much of a stiff upper lip.'

Douglas replaced his glasses. Fitzroy peered up at him. 'Ah, that's better. I can see what I'm about now. Can I have another drink?'

Douglas gave him one, and Fitzroy said: 'Hadn't you better be going? The Huns must be looking for you everywhere by now.'

'I'm not going without you,' Douglas told him quietly. 'I'm just trying to work out the best way of lashing you to a motor bike, that's all.'

'Callum, don't be a bloody fool!' Fitzroy's voice was full of strength. 'I'd be nothing but a damned burden to you. Besides, I don't know how long I can last.'

'He's right, boss,' Conolly said. Douglas rounded on him.

'Of course he's bloody well right! I was just thinking –'

He left the sentence unfinished. His thoughts had been busy with the information Fitzroy possessed about the location of the Allied landings, information which, if the Germans captured him and tore it from him, could throw the invasion into jeopardy.

Fitzroy knew exactly what was passing through the SAS officer's mind, and smiled. 'You've no need to worry, Callum. They won't get anything out of me. It won't be long now, anyway.'

'Callum, look!' It was Colette who spoke. She had been looking across the countryside, through shreds of mist that still clung to the valleys.

'There's a cottage over there, about a mile away,' she said. 'If we can get Major Fitzroy to it . . .'

'I'll get myself to it,' Fitzroy said. 'Just get me up, will you?'

Resignedly, assisted by Conolly, Douglas helped Fitzroy to his feet. He stood there swaying for a moment, then seemed to find his equilibrium. He took a few steps towards a hole in the hedge, where a gate had once been, then turned to face the others, who were watching him with grave expressions.

'I'll be off, then,' he said simply. 'Don't worry about me. It's the only sensible thing to do.'

He turned away again and set off through the neighbouring field at a stumbling walk, his damaged arm sticking out at an angle. Douglas picked up Fitzroy's German helmet from the road and threw it into the ditch, among the undergrowth. Brough had checked the motor cycles and found that, astonishingly, none had sustained any damage. In a low voice, Douglas gave the order to mount up.

Fitzroy looked back only once, as he heard the motor cycles roar off along the lane. Then he set his face towards the distant cottage once more and trudged on doggedly. The morphine tablet had numbed the pain, but it had also made him drowsy. He stumbled often as he walked, and twice he fell, rising again with an effort. It would have been very easy just to lie there in the wet grass, and sleep. Blood was already soaking through his bandages.

With a supreme effort of will, he kept on going. Within a couple of hundred yards of his goal he fell again, and this time his efforts to rise failed. Dimly, he realized that he had lost his glasses. Kneeling, he scrabbled around frantically in the grass with his good hand, but could not find them.

Putting his weight on his sound arm, he dragged himself on towards the cottage, now just a grey blur in his line of vision. He had lost all sense of time, and the cottage seemed to grow no bigger. In the end he crawled on blindly, leaving a patchy trail of blood behind him.

His head came into violent contact with something, stopping his progress immediately. It was a post of some kind. He put his arm around it, supporting himself. A strong, pungent smell reached his nostrils. Close by, something moved. A terrible face swam into partial focus, grey and horned, with long, yellowish teeth. For an awful moment Major Walter Fitzroy – a man with no particular religious convictions – believed that he had died and gone to hell.

Then the goat bleated at him, and a soundless spasm of laughter shook Fitzroy's body just before he passed out.

He came round coughing, in protest against the fiery liquid

93

that was being forced between his lips. Someone was doing something to his injured arm.

He opened his eyes. He was lying on a settee and a boy of about fourteen was bending over him, a cup of cognac in his hands. He straightened up and stepped back a pace.

Fitzroy turned his head. A grey-haired woman was winding fresh bandages around his arm. He was glad that he had been unconscious when she removed the old ones.

She completed her task, then, seeing that he was awake, stood up and looked at him. There was an unspoken question in her gaze.

Fitzroy told her who he was. She nodded, still unspeaking. The boy came forward again and gave him some more brandy. This time he relished the spirit. It felt good as it coursed down towards his stomach, both soothing and strengthening him.

'*Restez tranquille, Monsieur,*' the woman said. Her voice was hoarse, as though she suffered from some chest complaint. She nodded to the boy and together they went out of the room, closing the door behind them.

Presently she returned, carrying a bowl of broth, which she began to spoon-feed to the injured man. Fitzroy expressed his gratitude between mouthfuls and asked her if the boy was her son. She nodded.

'Yes, *Monsieur*. I have sent him for help. You need assistance; there is a doctor in a nearby village. He will tend to your hurts.'

Fitzroy felt apprehensive, but realized that he was completely in the woman's hands. He was in no fit state to go anywhere, not until his wounds were healed.

He had not slept at all the night before, and this fact, together with the brandy and the broth, overcame the throbbing pain in his arm. His head lolled to one side and he dozed off. The woman sat on a stool close by and watched him as he writhed fitfully and muttered in his sleep. She felt sorry for this strange, bedraggled and badly hurt man, and glad that she had been able to bring him a little comfort.

She recalled her son's errand, and for the tenth time

tortured herself with the question of whether she had done the right thing. But, she told herself, there had really been no choice.

Fitzroy awoke to a vicious slap across the face. The shock made him move sharply, and he cried out as the pain in his arm clutched at him.

A tough-looking, steel-helmeted German stared down at him. He carried a Schmeisser machine-pistol, which was pointed at Fitzroy's chest. More Germans crowded into the room. The woman stood in a corner of the room, ashen-faced and wringing her hands. There were tears on her cheeks.

'Forgive me, *Monsieur*!' she cried. 'They have my husband.'

She came forward and approached the German officer, a captain. Her hands were clasped in supplication. 'In God's name, you will release him now? I beg of you. . .'

The German pushed her roughly aside. 'Silence, woman, or you will join him!'

Fitzroy sat up painfully, his head swimming. He could not find it in himself to blame the woman. She certainly did not deserve to be treated roughly. He opened his mouth to speak to the captain in German, then thought better of it. It would perhaps be better not to reveal that he spoke their language.

'My name is Fitzroy,' he said slowly and distinctly, in English. 'I am a major in the British Army. I demand to be treated in accordance with my rank, and also in accordance with the articles of the Geneva Convention.'

The German sneered at him, and answered in passable but heavily-accented English. 'So, Major. Then where is your uniform? I do not see it. I see only that you are wearing civilian clothing. You are therefore a spy, and will be shot.'

Fitzroy was thankful that he had earlier shed the camouflage smock taken from one of the dead motor cyclists. Had he been found wearing that, he told himself, he would probably have been dragged out and shot there and then.

The German suddenly shot out a powerful hand and seized Fitzroy's jacket, dragging him to his feet. He pushed his face to within a few inches of the Englishman's. Abstractedly, Fitzroy thought: his breath smells of stale garlic.

'You do not look like an English Commando,' the German growled, 'but what else can you be, Major Fitzroy? Bah!'

He let go of the jacket, and Fitzroy fell back on to the settee. The pain in his arm was unbearable, but he forced himself not to show it. Time for the stiff upper lip, Walter old chap, he said to himself. Don't let these bastards see you're shit scared.

'We will shoot you anyway,' the German officer declared. 'We have no time to waste on you!'

He turned and snapped an order. Two of his men came forward and roughly manhandled Fitzroy to his feet. They dragged him across the room and outside into the yard.

Through the haze of his short-sightedness, he saw that two army vehicles, a truck and a *Kubelwagen* – the latter emitting faint squawking noises from an unseen radio set – were parked on the dirt road that led up to the cottage.

The Germans pushed Fitzroy up against the wall of an outhouse and moved away. He was barely able to stand. He would have liked to come to attention, to meet what was coming with some dignity, but if he placed his feet together he knew that he would fall. Instead, he leaned back against the wall, trying hard not to tremble.

In the background, he heard the sound of the woman crying.

Three German soldiers marched up and faced Fitzroy from a distance of ten yards. The officer stood off to one side. He issued a curt command and the three soldiers brought up their Schmeissers.

Fitzroy was quite calm. He wondered what it would feel like, then realized that he would probably not feel anything at all.

In the *Kubelwagen*, the radio continued to crackle. A soldier with headphones on was bending over it. Suddenly, he tore off his headset and gave an urgent shout. *Herr Hauptmann! Der Brite darf nicht erschossen sein!*

'*Was!*' The German officer swung round, outraged by the peremptory nature of the order from a mere private soldier. The latter scrambled out of the *Kubel*, straightening his forage cap, and ran up to the captain, crashing his heels together in front of him. The stunned Fitzroy heard what passed between them.

'Excuse me, *Herr Hauptmann*,' the wireless operator said. 'I humbly beg to report that, according to your orders, I informed headquarters of the capture of the British officer. I also beg to report that I have just received the following message from HQ.' His voice assumed a monotone as he quoted. '"The British officer is to come to no harm. He is required for urgent interrogation by the *Abwehr* and is to be taken with all speed to the interrogation centre in Bayeux." That is the message, *Herr Hauptmann*.'

'Bayeux? Good God, that's over a hundred kilometres away, even as the crow flies,' the officer snarled. 'Who issued these orders, anyway? Field Marshal Rommel himself?'

The soldier flinched before the officer's anger. 'No, sir. The field marshal has departed for Germany, I understand. The order was issued by General Speidel.'

The officer's wrath subsided a little. 'Well, I suppose we had better do what he wants.' He turned to the three armed soldiers. 'Put down your weapons,' he ordered. 'The Englishman lives, at least for the time being.'

Fitzroy just had time to hear the German's final words before he collapsed, senseless, on the soggy ground.

The countryside seemed to be crawling with the enemy. For nearly seventy miles Douglas and his small band had worked their way steadily across Normandy, a few miles at a stretch, following cart tracks and crossing open fields, avoiding all main roads as far as possible.

The weather had continued to favour them, but by mid-afternoon the grey clouds had risen and begun to disperse, opening the way for any German spotter aircraft that might be on the lookout for the fugitives. A few miles south of Lisieux, they had ditched the motor cycles and German clothing in a river and continued on foot, moving cautiously through picturesque valleys that were dotted with little white farms and inhabited by herds of meandering cows.

Douglas, Conolly and Brough lay among bracken at the edge of a wood. The others, secure in a thicket deeper among the trees, were catching some sleep. To the west, the sun, a welcome sight after the rain and grey skies of the preceding days, was sinking towards the horizon.

The wood stood astride a ridge, about five hundred feet above sea level. It was one of a series of ridges and hills that encircled Lisieux, and from it the SAS men had a clear view of the ancient city, with its spires and contrasting mixtures of red and grey stone. The city lay at the confluence of a network of roads and railway lines, and it was the traffic that passed along these that occupied Douglas's attention.

The fields below the ridge were criss-crossed with tank tracks. They were fresh, and they led away from a main road to various points in surrounding low-lying woods. Dozens of soldiers were at work in the fields, spreading freshly-cut grass over the track marks.

Douglas panned Conolly's binoculars across the scene and gave a running commentary to the Irishman, who was making notes.

'Looks like a full armoured division,' he said. 'They're camouflaging those tracks well; they will be invisible from the air. There seems to be a fuel dump in that small wood over on the right, too; I've seen at least three tankers go into it.' He consulted his map, and gave Conolly a series of references. He made a few more observations, then, accompanied by the other two, crept back into the trees. Once they were well clear of the edge of the wood, they stopped and conferred over what they had seen.

'I only hope that Mitch can make contact with those – what d'you call 'em? – those Ascension people tonight,' Douglas said. 'That Panzer division is well placed to go into action anywhere between the Seine estuary and Caen, within a few hours. It has obviously just moved up, and it's pretty well certain that our people don't know it's there. If we can call in the bombers in time –'

'It's very well dispersed,' Conolly interrupted. 'It would need a precision attack in daylight.'

'A job for the Yanks, then,' Brough commented.

'Maybe. It's the time factor that worries me, though. We can't do a damn' thing until the early hours of the morning. That's when the RAF Ascension planes fly their sorties over the Channel, according to Colette.'

Conolly looked hard at Douglas. 'The time factor, you said. Look, boss, it seems to me that you know more about this coming invasion than you've admitted so far. Can you tell us how much time we've got?'

Douglas thought for a few moments, then said: 'Well, it can't do much harm to tell you now, I suppose. I don't know the precise timing, but Major Fitzroy told me this morning that it would come within forty-eight hours. My own guess is that the invasion will take place the day after tomorrow, at dawn on the sixth of June.'

'Roll on,' Stan Brough said fervently. 'What I wouldn't give for a mug of tea and a bacon sandwich!'

'Me, too,' Douglas agreed. 'But don't forget – there'll be half the German army between us and the invasion, when it does take place. We'll have two alternatives: either we try to filter through the enemy lines and link up with our own chaps, or we stay put and wait for them to come to us. Maybe we can do a bit of damage, as well.'

They went back to join the others in the lengthening shadows. Most of them, including Mitchell, were already awake; the Rhodesian was checking his radio. He grunted as Conolly handed him the notes he had made.

'It'll take a while to encypher this lot,' he said. 'Better get cracking now, before the light goes completely. I'll start transmitting at oh-two-hundred.'

'Right,' Douglas said. 'We're going to get a bit of sleep. Wake us at midnight, Mitch.'

Douglas took a long drink from his water bottle and sucked a morsel of chocolate from his supply. Water, thankfully, had presented no problem during their journey, for they had passed numerous streams in their wanderings, but their rations were almost exhausted and hunger was an ever-present nagging ache. It would have been easy enough to live

99

off the land, for there was plenty of game in the woods; the problem was that they dared not light a fire for fear of discovery, and they were not yet desperate enough to eat raw meat.

Douglas finished his chocolate, sat back against a tree trunk and let his chin fall forward on his chest. His scalp, crusted as it was with dried blood, felt as though it were in the grip of a vice, but at least it had stopped hurting. Colette had wanted to look at it, but he had refused; there would be time enough for that later. Meanwhile, as long as it did not trouble him unduly, it was best left alone.

It was Olds who shook him awake. 'Midnight, sir,' he said. 'Mitch would like a word with you.'

Douglas rose stiffly and went over to join the Rhodesian, who told him that all was ready.

'I want to transmit from the northern edge of the wood, though,' he said. 'The trees can blanket the signal, under certain conditions. Another thing – I'll need a light to read the code.'

'We'll improvise something,' Douglas told him. 'Jackets, jumpers, that sort of thing – like reading under the bedclothes with a torch when you were a kid. We'd better all come with you, in case there's any trouble.'

They got their things together and trekked off through the woods. They had no need of a compass to get their bearings; the sky was clear and the Great Bear, directly overhead, pointed the way to the Pole Star. The stars were the only light, for the new moon had yet to make its appearance.

They came to a spot at the edge of the wood and set about rigging up a light-proof shelter in which Mitchell could use a small torch to read his codes. Below their vantage point, the darkened, rolling land stretched away to the Normandy coast, fifteen miles distant. There was no sound; it was as though the whole countryside was brooding, waiting in expectation and apprehension for what was soon to happen.

Waiting in darkness was always the worst. At last, after an age, Mitchell announced in a whisper that he was going to begin transmitting. He crawled into his shelter, which had been created by bending a few thin branches, implanting both ends in the ground and draping clothing thickly over them. The aerial of Mitchell's radio protruded through a jacket sleeve.

Mitchell went on transmitting for more than an hour, sending out the same coded messages over and over again. Finally, he closed down the radio, switched off his torch and crept backwards out of the shelter. His voice, as he addressed Douglas, was laden with dejection.

'No acknowledgement,' he said. 'I was transmitting blind the whole time. Not a damned thing.'

Douglas felt his heart sink, but he tried to sound encouraging. 'Never mind, Mitch. You did your best. You never know – someone might have heard you.'

Someone had. A few miles away, in the village of Livarot, the initial burst of coded transmission had roused a bored German signaller from his torpor. He was sitting in a radio truck, headphones in place, his job to detect any transmissions that might be the work of the French Resistance.

This transmission certainly sounded as though it came into that category, and moreover it was not too far away.

Still listening, he turned to his colleague, who was trying to read a novel in the dim light. 'Otto, I'm getting something! Get hold of number two post, fast, and see if they're picking it up also. Maybe we can get a fix on it.'

Quickly, the other German called up the crew of a similar vehicle, stationed on the other side of Lisieux. Yes, they told him, they were also picking up transmissions, but they could not make head or tail of them. They had already got a rough bearing: one-nine-zero degrees, true.

The signaller in the first radio truck reached up and turned a handle in the roof. As he swivelled it, the transmission alternately strengthened and faded. The loop aerial above the truck, which was linked to a compass face, showed that the transmission was at its most powerful on a bearing of three-five-zero degrees.

Otto, bent over a map, plotted two lines on it, each one following the bearing registered by the radio trucks. The two

101

lines crossed south of Lisieux. He drew a circle around the spot.

Then he turned his dial to a certain frequency, picked up his microphone, and issued a full alert to the headquarters of the 21st Panzer Division, whose tanks were stationed almost exactly in the area where the lines met.

CHAPTER NINE

For the hundredth time, Douglas cursed his own stupidity.

They should have put several miles between themselves and the wood as soon as Mitchell had finished making his radio transmission. Instead, their senses dulled by weariness, they had stayed where they were – and now they were trapped.

With the coming of dawn, Olds had set out to make a reconnaissance of the land all around the wood. As he moved along the perimeter of the trees, careful to keep under cover, the same sight had met his eyes on all sides: German patrols, dozens of them, moving through the surrounding valleys. Most of the patrols had tracker dogs with them, and Olds knew that if it had not been for the soaking grass, which had effectively disguised any scent left by the SAS party, the enemy would have hit upon their hiding place long before now.

The Germans were already beginning to search some of the neighbouring woods, mainly those to the south, as the sun climbed above the trees. The search seemed to be following a definite pattern, with several patrols forming two arms of a pincer whose points eventually joined to make a long, extended line.

It took a long time for this to happen, for the Germans were being very slow and very thorough, but as the day wore on the line swung about and began to move inexorably northward, its progress bringing it towards the wood on the ridge where Douglas and his party sheltered.

By late afternoon the Germans, having paused to search some farmhouses in the neighbourhood, had reached the foot of the slope that led up to the ridge. On either flank, more patrols extended to envelop the wood.

Only on one side, the side facing the spot where the Panzer division was encamped, were no enemy troops in evidence, although Douglas had no doubt that they were there, in the woods where the tanks were hidden. To try and escape down that long, exposed slope would be suicide, at least in daylight.

After dark, there might just be a slim chance that they could slip away by that route. The Germans, Douglas was certain, would call off their search at nightfall, but that was still a long way off.

Their immediate salvation, he decided, lay in concealment. As soon as Olds brought him news of the search, Douglas had ordered his small group to dig foxholes at intervals along the edge of the wood, just inside the trees, on the side overlooking the tank laager. Each foxhole was to be shared by two people, to provide mutual support if a German soldier stumbled on them. As there were nine in Douglas's party, he stationed Sansom up a tree, well hidden among the branches; from that position he could wreak silent and effective havoc with his crossbow if need be.

The discovery of one foxhole by the enemy would be the signal for them all to open fire with whatever weapons they had at their disposal. They all, with the exception of Colette, still had their MP-40s, with several clips of ammunition, and a few hand-grenades between them.

Colette was to share Douglas's foxhole. He wished to have her close to him, not because of what he felt for her, but for another and much grimmer reason. He did not intend to let her be taken alive by the Germans. Better death, than inevitable torture and, if she survived that, a concentration camp.

They camouflaged their foxholes with brushwood, twigs and grass, as they had been taught, and settled down in them as best they could. Sansom visited each one, carefully making sure that the camouflage was in place, before taking up station in his tree.

They waited, guns cocked with safety catches on, grenades within easy reach. The shadows were lengthening; cloud was coming up from the south-west once more, a great bank of it, driven before a freshening wind. Soon it would obscure the sun, bringing an early dusk. So much the better, thought Douglas.

There were voices among the trees, somewhere up front. A dog barked; boots crunched in the undergrowth. In their foxholes, Douglas and the others froze into effigies, breathing very slowly and quietly. Beside him, Douglas felt Colette begin to tremble.

The sounds were very close now. Most of them Douglas could identify, but there was one he could not, and he was puzzled by it. It was a dull, rumbling sound, and it grew louder with every passing second. Moreover, it was coming from behind him.

Shouts of alarm echoed through the woods. A whistle shrilled three times. There were crashing sounds, as though men were running away, or throwing themselves headlong in the undergrowth.

Sansom, high in his tree, had seen what was coming for some time, but for obvious reasons had been unable to alert the others.

Heading directly towards the wood, flying at a height of only a few thousand feet, was the biggest formation of heavy bombers he had ever seen. There must have been over a hundred of them, all four-engined Avro Lancasters, and they seemed to be heading directly for him, personally. High above weaved their fighter escort, which seemed hardly necessary in view of this massive show of strength.

Sticks of bombs fell from the leading wave of Lancasters. They curved down towards the valley below, and the tanks hidden among the trees. Sansom put both arms around a tree branch and clung on grimly.

The earth exploded. Boiling clouds of smoke mushroomed up as the thousand-pounders detonated. The concussions were shattering, fearsome. Sansom's tree shook violently and it was all he could do to retain his hold.

For those in the ground, the effect was even worse. Beneath them, the soil trembled and heaved and shook as one series of hammer-blows after another smote the valley. Added to the terrible thud and blast of the bombs now was the sharper crack of exploding ammunition, as 88-mm shells and machine-gun bullets detonated in the carcases of ruined Tiger tanks. Sansom swallowed hard as he saw a tank turret, complete with gun, sail high above the trees, turning over and over before crashing back to earth.

The pounding went on and on, numbing the senses. The bombers were right on target, slamming their loads of high explosive into the woods where the *Panzers* were concealed.

In Lisieux, the good townspeople cowered in their cellars and wondered if the end of the world had come, as their windows shattered and tiles slid from their roofs.

In his foxhole, next to Lambert, Mitchell smiled happily to himself. It could only have been his radio signal that had brought this about; and if Ascension had picked up the message about this concentration of enemy armour, it must also have received those telling of Rommel's absence on leave, and of the northward movement across the Seine of the 112th Panzer Division.

As the bombers released their cargoes into the inferno below, they wheeled as though on parade, turning to the left in stately ranks and heading back towards the coast. A few bursts of light flak pursued them belatedly, but they were out of its range.

The roar of the engines dwindled as the Lancasters thundered into the distance. Stan Brough, dazed by the repeated concussions, envied the crews; piece of cake, old boy, and back to the bacon and eggs. Then he told himself that he was being unfair. Too many of the poor buggers never made it back.

The valley was obscured by rolling clouds of smoke, shot with flame. Here and there, a delayed-action bomb detonated with a thump, sending a fresh fountain of smoke and earth into the air.

In the wood where the SAS group lay, there was a sudden commotion. German soldiers burst from among the trees, dashing past the foxholes and on down the slope towards the carnage below. An iron-shod boot struck the burly Olds in the small of the back, causing an involuntary grunt, but the German responsible careered on, unaware that he had just trodden on a human being.

Douglas and the others lay quite still for several minutes. Then, very carefully, Douglas raised his head and looked around him in the half-light. As he turned, he saw for the first time the havoc the bombers had wrought. As the darkness gathered, the scene appeared even more hellish. The whole valley floor seemed to be on fire; ammunition continued to explode, and flares, cooked off by the heat, soared into the sky in multi-coloured firework displays.

Tanks which had escaped the holocaust crawled around the valley floor, their crews driving them at top speed out of danger. Douglas counted them as they formed up in a line on the adjacent road, and calculated that the division had lost about a third of its effective strength. There were still a great many Tiger tanks left intact – enough to make a decisive impact if they were thrown into the coming battle.

'They didn't get the fuel dump,' remarked Conolly, who had also emerged from his foxhole. Douglas saw that the Irishman was right; there was no sign of damage to the clump of trees into which he had seen the succession of fuel tankers vanish earlier in the day.

'Liam,' Douglas said after a few moments of thought, 'what's the range of a Tiger, fully fuelled?'

'Well, we managed about sixty miles in the one we captured in Tunisia, if you remember. I'd say seventy miles at the outside. You'd soon use up seventy miles' worth of diesel around here.'

Douglas knew what Conolly meant. The *bocage* country of Normandy was a spider's web of narrow, winding roads, flanked by tall double hedgerows. In some places, tanks would have to make wide detours to avoid the so-called *prairies marécageuses*, extensive tracts of swampland.

'Right,' he said. 'We'll wait until it gets really dark, then slip down there and tickle 'em up a bit. Barber, where are you?'

Barber came up out of the shadows. 'How much plastic have you got left?' Douglas asked. Barber said that he still had half a dozen charges.

'Enough to blow up a fuel dump?'

'Depends on how the fuel is stored,' Barber told him. 'But I could certainly make a hole in it.'

'Then we'll do it. I think the Huns will be too busy to worry about us for the next few hours.'

The Germans were still fighting the fires well after midnight, their task complicated by exploding ammunition, when Douglas and his men set out on their mission. They were all taking part except for Colette and Lambert; Colette was worn out and Lambert was complaining of a sprained ankle, so Douglas had decided to leave them in the wood. If the explosives party encountered trouble and had to make a dash up the slope, the pair in the wood could provide covering fire.

Douglas and his six companions kitten-crawled diagonally down the slope, their MP-40s cradled across their arms as they pulled themselves along on their elbows. Douglas had worked out that the best way of approaching the copse that held the enemy's fuel was to make for the tall hedge that bordered the road, and use it as shelter. The tanks were on the other side, a little farther along the road.

They crawled on, stopping every so often to watch and listen. They reached the hedge and paused again, lying prone in the neighbouring ditch. Douglas found to his dismay that it was filled with tangled thorns, which lacerated his face and hands as he squirmed through them. It was a relief when at last he reached the edge of the copse and was able to pull himself away from the clutches of the thorns. He could feel blood running down his cheeks, mingling with the dirt which he had smeared on his face for camouflage.

Light from the fires that still burned across the valley flickered through the trees. They glinted on metal. Douglas crept forward and peered round a tree trunk. A huge fuel bowser, its hull camouflaged in a splinter pattern of green and black, stood in a clearing. He could just make out several more, parked beyond it. The vehicles did not appear to be guarded.

Douglas stood up slowly, blending himself against the tree, and motioned to the men who followed him. Like dark phantoms they spread out, flitting from tree to tree as they approached the bowsers.

A figure materialized beside Douglas. 'Okay, sir?' Barber whispered.

'Okay. Off you go, and watch your step.'

Barber, clutching the pack that contained his explosives, dropped flat on his belly and slithered away towards the nearest bowser. Douglas saw him vanish underneath it. He began ticking off the seconds mentally, a habit he had developed over the years in situations such as this.

The count had reached two hundred and forty when Douglas heard voices. They seemed to be coming from somewhere on his left, from the western side of the copse.

The voices grew louder, and Douglas released the safety catch of his MP-40. He could see dark silhouettes now, moving towards him through the trees. He counted eight men, and reasoned that they were probably the crews of the fuel tankers, called away to help fight the fires the bombers had started.

'That's it, sir.' The hoarse whisper at his elbow made him jump. 'Let's go,' Barber added. 'I've set a two-minute delay.'

Bent double, they ran back through the trees, the others joining them as they went. Behind them, a shout rang out:

'*Halt! Wer da?*'

They ran on, putting all their energy into it. The harsh command to halt came again, accompanied a moment later by a rattle of sub-machine-gun fire. Bullets chopped bark off the trees behind the fleeing men.

They burst out of the copse, pursued by more bullets. There were shouts close at hand, and Douglas saw a cluster of Germans heading towards them from the right.

Conolly saw them too, and sent a burst of MP-40 fire in their direction, firing from the hip. Two fell. The others fired back, but the dark shapes of the SAS men were hidden against the background of the hedge and they were firing blind. Their shots went wide.

There was perhaps a hundred yards between them and their pursuers, but Douglas knew that they would never make it up the slope without sustaining casualties. He yelled 'Keep going!' to the others and dropped on one knee, chopping at the enemy in short bursts.

Brough's voice rang out through the darkness. 'Fall back, sir! I'll cover you!'

The sergeant-major's gun hammered and Douglas bolted back to drop on one knee a few yards behind him. Mitchell joined him, then the three of them fell back to be covered in turn by the other four. Olds saw one of the Germans bring back his arm, ready to throw a grenade, and coolly shot him down. The grenade went off with a muffled crack, and there were cries of pain.

The Germans were spreading out, trying to encircle them. One, braver than the rest, came forward, crouching in a zig-zag run, firing as he went. Close to Douglas there was a grunt, as though someone had been punched in the stomach. He raised his gun, sighted carefully and fired. The German collapsed in a sprawling slide and lay still.

Douglas turned. Someone was lying on the ground a few paces behind him, moaning softly. Conolly was bending over him.

'It's Sansom,' he cried. 'He's badly hit. We've –'

Conolly's voice was interrupted by a succession of muffled thuds, followed by a massive roar. Night turned into day as the bowsers in the copse exploded. A great mushroom of burning fuel oil burst upwards in a wave of light and heat. Startled, the Germans turned their attention away from the fugitives.

'Give me a hand, Liam,' Douglas panted. 'Let's get him up the slope, under cover.'

Olds appeared at Douglas's elbow. 'I'll do it, sir,' he said. 'You keep the Jerries' heads down.'

The burly ex-farm labourer picked up Sansom's body as though it were made of feathers and swung it over his shoulder in a fireman's lift. He set off up the slope at a shambling run, the others falling back behind him. Some desultory shots crackled after them, but the explosion of the bowsers had thrown the Germans off balance and it was a good minute before one of their NCOs was able to rally them and order the pursuit to continue.

They reached the shelter of the trees. Colette appeared out of the undergrowth, full of concern, as Olds gently laid down Sansom's body. She felt the side of his neck, then stood up to face Douglas.

'He's dead,' she said simply.

Douglas made no reply. There was no time for regret now. In a few minutes they would probably all be dead.

Mitchell handed Colette Sansom's MP-40, which he had picked up. 'Do you know how to use this, Miss?' he asked. She nodded and lay down at the edge of the wood, in line with the rest of them, her gun pointing down the slope.

The Germans were advancing cautiously, in short dashes. Douglas decided to keep them guessing about the size of the opposition.

'Keep moving from place to place,' he called out. 'Make 'em think there are a lot of us. Hold your fire until I give the word.'

They had one advantage. The figures of the enemy soldiers stood out clearly against the flames that roared from the blazing copse. One group of about ten men, some distance ahead of the rest, had approached to within fifty yards of the wood on the ridge.

'Group of men at two o'clock,' Douglas said, his voice calm. 'Fire!'

The MP-40s chattered and the dark shapes of the enemy soldiers wilted away. Two escaped the withering fire, and ran back down the slope in search of cover. Another, smaller group made a dash forward, and met a similar fate. Following Douglas's instructions, the SAS men changed their positions and awaited the next assault.

Douglas tossed aside an empty magazine and replaced it with a full one. It was his last.

'Try and conserve your ammo,' he ordered. 'Try and break up their attacks with grenades.'

He knew that their position was hopeless. In minutes their ammunition would be exhausted; all they could do was to retreat deep into the wood and do their best to conceal themselves, then try and get away after daylight. With sick certainty, he knew that they would never make it.

There was a deep drone of aero-engines overhead. The sound had been present for some minutes, but Douglas had taken no notice of it, having had the more pressing matter of survival on his mind.

Then he saw the parachutes. There were dozens, scores of them, their canopies redly reflected the glow of the fires in the valley. They drifted slowly down out of the broken clouds, extending as far as the eye could see. Flashes came from the dark figures that dangled beneath them, and the sky was filled with what sounded like the crackle of small-arms fire.

Stunned, Colette and the SAS men stood there in silence, staring at the spectacle unfolding before them. The Germans were running back down the slope, blazing away at the descending figures. On the road, the tanks were starting up their engines.

One of the parachutes came to earth a few yards down the slope. The figure beneath it lay still. Douglas and Conolly dashed forward to help what they thought to be an injured man. A few moments later, they faced one another over the inert shape, amazement in their expressions.

'It's a dummy,' said Conolly. 'A bloody dummy, with firecrackers strung around it. What the hell –'

'Look,' Douglas said, pointing. 'Look at that.'

Away to the north, the whole horizon was lit up by rippling flashes. They ran to and fro, like horizontal lightning. The flashes continued, unceasing, as wave after wave of Allied bombers pounded the German fortifications of Hitler's Atlantic Wall.

It was a full two minutes before the rolling thunder of the explosions reached the small group by the edge of the wood.

The full-scale assault from the air could mean only one thing. For the first time since they had met in France, Douglas took Colette in his arms and hugged her to him.

CHAPTER TEN

The Lancasters flew steadily on over the Channel, heading for a point that lay midway between Le Havre and Dieppe. There were eight of them, flying in two lines, each consisting of four aircraft abreast, with four miles between each bomber and eight miles between the lines.

The bombers belonged to the celebrated No 617 Squadron, which had shattered the Ruhr dams just over a year earlier. Their crews were among the best and most experienced in the Royal Air Force.

The Lancasters were carrying out a strange manoeuvre. Ever since they had formed up over the English coast they had been creeping across the Channel by flying a series of oblong patterns, each oblong measuring precisely eight miles by two. At exact intervals, on each of the eight-mile legs, the Lancasters dropped bundles from their bomb-bays. The bundles came apart in mid-air and showered masses of tinfoil towards the waters of the Channel, far below. The bundles had to be dropped at a rate of twelve per minute.

Each oblong flight pattern was a mile ahead of the previous one, the Lancasters flying with beautiful precision at three thousand feet. The height had to be precise, so that the bundles of tinfoil – known as 'window' – would not disperse too widely before they hit the water.

On the screens of the enemy's coastal radar stations, the reflections produced by the tinfoil bundles looked exactly like a mighty force of ships, moving across the Channel at a speed of about seven knots.

To produce larger echoes on the enemy radar with the passage of time, fostering the illusion that a huge fleet was heading towards the French coast, the size of the 'window' bundles was gradually increased. As an extra precaution, in case the ruse was detected and analyzed for what it was by enemy airborne radar, a small force of harbour defence boats and air-sea rescue launches kept station beneath the orbiting Lancasters. These vessels carried a device known as 'Moonshine', which picked up enemy radar pulses, amplified them and re-transmitted them, giving a 'solid' radar impression of a large concentration of ships forging slowly ahead.

The boats also towed 'Filberts', twenty-nine-foot-long barrage balloons with radar reflectors built inside their envelopes. Each 'Filbert' produced a radar echo similar to that of a 10,000-ton ship.

The Lancasters' mission – code-named Operation Taxable – ended at a point exactly ten miles from Cap d'Antifer, within range of the German coastal gun batteries. As the bombers turned for home, their accompanying boats moored their 'Filbert' floats and laid a smokescreen, at the same time broadcasting recorded sounds over powerful loudspeakers of large vessels dropping anchor.

Seventy miles to the north, a second force of aircraft and boats was carrying out a similar mission, Operation Glimmer, over the Straits of Dover off Boulogne. Dawn was beginning to break as this force also completed its task.

In the headquarters of the German Fifteenth Army, which controlled operations north of the Seine, there was confusion. Two-thirds of the German coastal radar stations had been knocked out, many of them in the heavy air attacks which had taken place during the night, but those which had survived intact between Le Havre and Boulogne were reporting what appeared to be two big invasion task forces, heading for separate points along the coast.

The order went out for the 112th Panzer Division, creeping northwards after crossing the Seine, to proceed to the coastal area with all possible speed to join other German forces in repelling the landings.

It seemed that Field Marshal Rommel had been right, after all, in his assumption that the Allies would push their invasion forces across the shortest Channel route.

In the redoubts along the coast, gun crews elevated the muzzles of their huge cannon, relying on co-ordinates passed to them by the radar stations. As dawn – a grey, windswept dawn – began to lighten the sky, they could see smoke drifting across the horizon to the north-west.

Within minutes, hundreds of shells were screeching down on the places where the coastal radar had indicated that the invasion fleets were lying. A holocaust of steel and high explosive ripped into the Channel, sending up forests of waterspouts.

It was a long time before the gunners realized that they had been the victims of a gigantic hoax, and that the sea was empty.

In a small, airless room in Bayeux a man sat strapped to a heavy metal chair. He was numb with pain, for although his tormentors had not physically tortured him, they had done nothing to tend his injured arm, and the continual jolting of the truck that had brought him here had driven him close to madness.

Time had no meaning. He had no idea how long he had been there; a day, a day and a half perhaps. There had been long periods of darkness, merciful periods, stripped brutally away by a douche of cold water in the face. The darkness had become grey, and at those times shadowy figures had been hovering about him.

There had been whispering voices; voices that never threatened, always cajoled. The voices were there again, sibilant and insistent.

'Come, Major Fitzroy, what is the point of resisting any longer? You are cold, and in pain. Think of it – a clean bed, a bath, nurses to tend your arm, food and drink. Just tell us when the invasion will come. Tell us where it will be. Just answer those two small questions, and then you can rest.'

The room suddenly trembled. Fitzroy's dazed and battered senses registered a series of deep concussions, merging into a continuous drum-roll of sound as they blended together. Dimly, he recognized the patterns of sticks of bombs, and something else; the jarring crump of heavy naval gunfire.

He managed to turn his head towards his interrogator, whose face he had never clearly seen. Moistening his swollen tongue, he just managed to squeeze out a few weak words before the darkness closed over him again.

'The invasion? If you listen very carefully, old boy, you might just be able to hear it.'

Most men were already awake when reveille sounded in the ships of the invasion armada that was descending on Normandy. Most, too, managed to force down some breakfast, knowing that it would be the last food they would get for some time.

Somewhere beyond the horizon, behind the coastal defences, American and British airborne troops had already been fighting hard for several hours, striving to secure a number of key objectives in conjunction with the assault from the sea. Here, too, subterfuge played its part; the dummy paratroops that had brought salvation to Douglas and his group had caused great confusion in the enemy's rear areas.

The fighting was bitter. When it was over, names such as St Mère Eglise and Pegasus Bridge would be indelibly printed in the pages of history.

The planners had given the invasion beaches picturesque names: Omaha and Utah, where the American divisions were to go ashore, Gold and Sword for the British, Juno for the Canadians.

The big LSIs – Landing Ships, Infantry – reached their lowering positions, some seven or eight miles off the French coast, and the assault battalions embarked in their landing craft – no mean feat in itself, for a heavy swell was running and the craft were tossed up and down like corks. Amphibious tanks wallowed in the sea like prehistoric monsters, ready to lend their firepower to the initial assault waves.

There were other tanks, too, specially modified to undertake various tasks of destruction. There was the Flail tank, designed to beat a path through minefields, the Bobbin, which could lay a path across mud or quicksand, the Petard, which mounted a 25-pound mortar that could blast a hole through pillboxes or sea walls, and the deadly Crocodile flame-thrower, which could pump four hundred gallons of liquid fire over a distance of a hundred and twenty yards. All these devices were intended to blast a path for the infantry across the beaches.

Visibility was poor as the assault craft and their supporting Tank Landing Craft began their run-in towards the beaches, with the coastline obscured by haze. A terrible blanket of noise lay over everything, as the warships of the naval task forces hurled their shells and rocket projectiles at the enemy positions that lay hidden in the murk and bombers thundered overhead, carpeting the areas behind the beaches with their bombs. A great pall of smoke rose over the battle areas.

It seemed impossible that anyone could have survived under that terrible weight of metal, but as the landing craft approached the beaches they were increasingly raked by artillery and small arms fire. Landing craft were hit in deep water, and men who jumped overboard were dragged down by their heavy loads to drown.

From beach to beach, there were strange contrasts. On Omaha Beach, the Americans – first ashore because of the difference in tidal levels along the coast – made their landing amid noise and flame and hellish gunfire, and suffered terrible casualties. Yet a few miles away, British troops approached Gold Beach in comparative calm, with no sign of enemy opposition behind the drifting smoke clouds.

The beach seemed to be completely deserted, and even when the troops jumped from their assault craft to wade through the surf there was still no enemy fire. The lack of opposition was unreal, almost eerie.

Then, after the troops had advanced two hundred yards, the beach suddenly exploded as the Germans opened up with everything they had – mortars, machine-guns, artillery. Here, it was the Petard and Flail tanks that came to the rescue, knocking out enemy pillboxes and blasting paths through the minefields, enabling the troops to fight their way off the beaches and take the high ground.

And so, on that Tuesday morning in June, 1944, the Allies returned to France, more than a quarter of a million individual stories merging into the greater whole that was known as D-Day.

The villa at Herrlingen was filled with the scent of flowers. It was Lucie Rommel's birthday, and gifts had poured in from friends and relatives.

Erwin Rommel was determined to make it a day to remember. He had shaved in his usual leisurely fashion, and now one of his house guests, a general's wife, was helping him to wrap presents he had bought for Lucie in Paris.

His lumbago still tugged at him, but he had made up his mind that he would never allow it to annoy him again. Had it not been for his lumbago, he would now almost certainly have been lying dead alongside poor Mercke.

He had wanted to stay, to supervise personally the hunt for the terrorists who had killed Mercke. It was Speidel who had persuaded him to leave as planned. Well, he thought, maybe Speidel had been right. The bespectacled general was competent enough to clear up the mess.

There was a knock on the door and a pretty housemaid came in. Rommel smiled at her; he liked to make his servants feel at ease. 'Yes, Karolina, what is it?'

'The field marshal is wanted on the telephone,' she told him respectfully.

'Thank you, Karolina.' Rommel straightened up from his task of wrapping Lucie's presents. 'Finish these off for me, Hildegard, if you would be so kind,' he said to his companion. 'That will be the Führer's adjutant – I am expecting a call from him.'

But the voice on the other end of the line was not that of Hitler's adjutant. It was General Speidel's. Despite the grave tidings he brought, Speidal's tone was as flat and imperturbable as ever.

'*Herr Feldmarschall*, the Allies have landed in Normandy,' Speidel said.

Rommel's tanned face suddenly turned white. 'What? Normandy, you say? Are they ashore anywhere else? Is it a diversion?'

'No, they are ashore at several places along the Normandy coast. There have apparently been diversionary measures elsewhere, but no other landing attempts. It is definitely Normandy, and nowhere else. Their troops and tanks are swarming ashore everywhere.'

'I will come back at once,' Rommel snapped. 'Are we counter-attacking?'

'We are resisting with the forces already in position,' Speidel said.

'But what about the armour?' Rommel was shouting now. 'Damn it, there are three Panzer divisions within striking distance of the coast! What about them?'

'One was severely damaged in a heavy British bombing attack last night,' Speidel informed him. 'I am holding the other two in reserve in case these landings are merely a feint. You yourself said that any assault on Normandy would be a diversionary measure, and that the real attack would fall on the Fifteenth Army,' he reminded Rommel succinctly.

Rommel repeated that he was returning immediately, and slammed down the receiver. He strode to the door and shouted for his valet. 'Tell Corporal Daniel to get my car ready. And ring Captain Lang. Tell him to meet me in Freudenstadt.'

Rommel hastily put on his uniform, and his valet, having done as his chief asked, packed a travelling bag. The field marshal bade goodbye to his wife, whose birthday celebrations now lay in ruins but who bore her husband's sudden departure without complaint. She had been a soldier's wife for too long to do otherwise.

Rommel picked up Lang, his aide, in Freudenstadt and they raced on towards the French border. Rommel's valet had packed some sandwiches and coffee and they ate as they went, stopping only in Reims for petrol and so that Rommel could telephone Speidel for the latest news. It was not good.

For the first time, Rommel learned how the Allies had used all manner of special equipment to punch their way through his Zone of Death, how they had attacked at low tide instead of high, as he had expected, and how their tanks had simply rolled through his obstacles – many of which had already been destroyed by Commandos – to blast the surviving strong-points with flame-throwers and explosive charges.

It was five o'clock in the afternoon when he telephoned from Reims, and still the Panzer divisions had not moved.

Back in the car, he was disconsolate. To Lang, he said: 'If the Allies succeed, the blame will fall on me. No matter how many other people have been guilty of misjudgement and mismanagement, it is I who will be the scapegoat. Oh, Lang, if only I had been there! Did I not say that the first day of the invasion would be the longest and most decisive day . . .'

It was ten o'clock before Rommel finally arrived at his headquarters, and was able to confer with his staff. He soon found that, short of going there personally, it was almost impossible to find out what was going on in Normandy. The German radio frequencies were being jammed, and many telephone lines had been severed by the French Resistance, who had emerged in great numbers during the night as soon as they heard the coded message that was the signal for the invasion.

Rommel spent a sleepless night, barking orders over the telephone when he finally did manage to get through to someone. He ordered the armoured divisions to attack at first light with all their available resources, which were dwindling rapidly under constant enemy air attack. British and American fighter-bombers, armed with rocket projectiles, were seeking out his tanks deep behind the battlefront and mauling them badly.

Above all, Rommel needed reserves of armour to meet the threat in Normandy. He decided that he could afford to withdraw one division, the 112th, from Fifteenth Army's command north of the Seine and commit it to action on the

Normandy front. That would still leave Fifteenth Army with three Panzer divisions with which to counter a fresh invasion across the Straits of Dover. This, Rommel was still convinced, was the enemy's trump card.

His last act that night was to order the 112th Panzer Division south.

That momentous day had also been a long one for Douglas and his group. They had spent the remainder of the night deep in the shelter of the wood in case the Germans renewed their hunt for them, but when they had returned to the perimeter of the trees when full daylight came it had been to find the valley empty.

Their first sad task after that had been to bury poor Sansom, who had shared so many dangers and adventures with the rest of them. They laid him in a shallow grave at the edge of the wood, in the shadow of a wild apple tree, and made a rough cross from branches to stand over him.

Douglas said a few words, and then, without looking back, they descended into the valley below. Smoke still drifted from the copse where the fuel bowsers had exploded.

The Germans had pulled out in a great hurry, leaving a considerable litter behind them. Douglas's first concern was to find some ammunition, and with this in mind he headed for the woods on the far side of the valley, where the Tiger tanks had been concealed.

It was only now, as they crossed the valley floor, that they were able to gain a full impression of the devastation created by the RAF bombers. There were craters everywhere, in many cases overlapping, and the air reeked of explosives. It was the first time they had witnessed the effects of a concentrated bombing attack on a small area. The enemy had removed their casualties, but Douglas fancied that a smell of death hung in the air. Perhaps it was no more than an illusion.

The sticks of bombs had smashed great swathes through the trees, and the smashed hulks of tanks lay among the splintered wood.

'Forget the tanks,' Douglas ordered. 'Their machine-guns use the wrong calibre of ammunition. Look out for trucks. That's where we're likely to find what we want.'

In the event, they found more than Douglas had bargained for. Probing deeper among the shattered trees, they came upon a set of tyre marks that seemed to end in a pile of tumbled tree trunks. Scrambling over them, they discovered a BMW truck that had escaped the fury of the bombing and which appeared to be completely intact, apart from a few splinter holes in its sides. The only problem was that it was completely blocked in by the tangle of trees that surrounded it.

Conolly wormed his way past the fallen trunks with difficulty and disappeared round the rear of the vehicle. A moment later, he let out a whoop of elation. 'Jackpot!' he called. 'Come and look at this lot!'

Douglas and the rest joined the Irishman, and stared in disbelief at the contents of the truck. It was piled high with boxes and crates containing all manner of food and drink. The full extent of the treasure trove revealed itself as Conolly broke open some of the boxes.

There were smoked hams, sausages, cheeses, jars of pickles and preserves, the latter mainly damsons. There were cases of wine and champagne, crates holding bottles of cognac carefully packed in straw. There were tins of cigarettes.

They stared at it all in awe. Conolly picked up a bottle of champagne and looked questioningly at Douglas. The latter shrugged.

'Why the hell not?' he said. 'Break a few open, Liam. We could all do with a drink, and a good feed, too. I've forgotten what it's like.'

Conolly eased the cork out of a champagne bottle. Foam welled down the sides and he handed it to Colette. She looked at it for a moment, savouring it, then said quietly, 'To Sansom,' before raising it to her lips.

They each took a bottle and raised it in silent tribute to their dead comrade. Barber drew apart from the rest and sat on a fallen tree trunk with his back to them. Sansom had been his friend.

They drank. The champagne was warm, but it tasted like nectar in their dry throats. Douglas looked at his bottle, and saw to his astonishment that it was already more than half empty. He felt a crazy urge to giggle, stifling it with difficulty.

Conolly was wandering around distributing sausage and ham, singing something in a quiet voice about a pig owned by a certain Rafferty as he did so. A little danger signal flashed in Douglas's head.

'We've got to take it easy on the booze, Liam. Food, that's one thing. Get some food into us.'

'That's right, boss. Lots and lots of luvverly grub. Fill our boots.'

Conolly looked at the truck thoughtfully. 'Bet somebody gets a bollocking for leaving this lot behind,' he said. 'Supplies for the officers' mess, I shouldn't wonder.'

'More likely some general's private hoard,' Douglas said, 'all packed up and ready to move.'

'Shame we can't take it with us,' mourned the usually stolid Olds, his speech a little slurred. Olds was unused to champagne and other alien tipples. 'Could live happily ever after off this lot.'

Stan Brough, who had gone off to snoop around the front of the truck, returned with a metal box, which he laid carefully at Douglas's feet. 'I come bearing gifts, O Master,' he said with champagne-induced jocularity, flipping back the lid of the box. It was filled with clips and nine-millimetre ammunition, the right calibre for their MP-40s.

'Stan, you're a bloody marvel,' Douglas breathed. 'Where did you find this?'

'It was in the cab,' Brough told him, 'under the passenger seat. Whoever was looking after this lot was obviously prepared to defend it – against looters, I imagine. There must have been a few ordinary lads who'd have liked to get their hands on it,' he added, with one soldier's sympathy for another.

Douglas looked at the sergeant-major. 'Stan,' he said, 'do you think there's any chance of getting the truck out of here?'

Brough shook his head slowly. 'It could be done, but it would take days, and a lot more muscle power than we've got. Anyway, there'd be little point. We wouldn't last five minutes on the roads; the whole rear area will be crawling with enemy patrols by now, on the lookout for paratroops.'

'I suppose you're right,' Douglas said. 'We've pulled off stunts with captured enemy vehicles in the past, and I suppose that it would be over-optimistic to think that we could do it again, and get away with it.' He smiled wearily. 'Never mind, though – at least we won't be short of rations, from now on.'

Conolly had opened a tin of cigarettes and was sniffing at its contents. 'Turkish,' he said appreciatively, taking one out and holding it under his nose. 'The owner of this little consignment certainly had taste.'

'Hand 'em round, Liam,' Douglas said. They all took one except Colette, who shook her head in refusal. Brough lit them with his ancient petrol lighter, a tool that had served them well on numerous occasions.

Douglas did not smoke very often, and the rich tobacco made his head swim a little as he inhaled. The week-old wound in his scalp was beginning to pain him again, but it was a healthy pain, as though everything was knitting together satisfactorily. There was none of the throbbing and soreness associated with infection.

Barber had also taken a cigarette. The combined effects of food, alcohol and tobacco seemed to have lifted his depression to some extent, and he had now turned to face the others, although he still sat some distance apart from them.

The explosives specialist dropped his half-smoked cigarette, ground it under his boot and got up from his tree trunk, stretching slowly. He strolled nonchalantly over to where Douglas was sitting, hands in pockets. Instead of stopping, he walked straight past, gazing at nothing in particular.

'Don't make any moves,' he said softly, his lips barely moving. 'We're being watched. Leave it to me.'

He passed by the side of the truck, stepping over the fallen trunks, and disappeared around the front end. Conolly, who had overheard Barber's remark, took some ham from the

125

back of the truck and went up to each of the others in turn, making a show of offering the food to them, and at the same time quietly repeating what Barber had said.

Several minutes went by. Douglas, leaning with his back to a tree, pretended to doze, the half-empty champagne bottle clutched in his hand. His MP-40 lay beside him; it would take only a second to take a clip of ammunition from the box and slam it into place.

There was a yelp of alarm and fright, followed by sounds of a scuffle, out of sight behind some fallen trees. Then Barber emerged, dragging a body behind him. He hoisted it over a tree trunk that lay in his path and dumped it on the ground in front of Douglas.

'Is he dead?' Douglas asked. Barber shook his head.

'No, I just thumped him. He'll come round in a minute or two.'

Douglas looked down at the senseless man, who lay flat on his back, arms outstretched. He was bearded and dirty, and had the shrunken-cheeked appearance of someone who had not eaten for a long time.

He was dressed in a worn German field-grey tunic, with baggy trousers tucked into jackboots. The tunic had black epaulettes, with a red border and a white stripe running across it. Apart from the German eagle on the left arm, the uniform was devoid of any other insignia.

Douglas asked Conolly, who was an expert on the enemy's badges, if he recognized the man's unit. The Irishman had to admit that he did not.

The man groaned and opened his eyes. He sat up and rocked backwards and forwards, massaging the back of his neck, then looked round him uncomprehendingly, his mouth open and showing broken teeth.

'Find out who he is and what he's doing, Liam,' Douglas ordered. Conolly spoke to the man in German and he answered in the same language, although haltingly and with many errors.

Conolly spoke to him for several minutes, then turned back to Douglas.

126

'Well, I'll be buggered,' he said in surprise. 'He's a Russian, or, to be more precise, a Ukrainian. He was very emphatic about the distinction. He's also a deserter, and there are others like him, not very far away.'

The man was looking longingly at the food and drink which Conolly had brought from the back of the truck. Saliva drooled from the corners of his mouth.

'Give him some, Liam,' Douglas said, 'but tell him to go easy. I don't want him passing out on us before we've found out more about him.'

Conolly gave the man a chunk of sausage and some champagne. They waited while he worried at the food like a hungry dog, taking long gulps of champagne in between mouthfuls. When he had finished, he gave Douglas and Conolly a pathetic look of gratitude. Then he bowed his head in his arms and burst into tears.

After a while, he calmed down a little and gave Conolly the rest of his story. It was a strange tale, and Douglas listened in fascination as Conolly translated.

The man was one of thousands of Ukrainians who, in 1941, had greeted the Germans as liberators when the *Wehrmacht* invaded Russia; for centuries, the Ukraine had been prostrated by Russian tyranny. He had enthusiastically joined a Ukrainian regiment, formed by the Germans for service on the eastern front, but the enthusiasm had turned sour amid the winter snows. There had been news, too, of German atrocities in the Ukraine, far worse than any perpetrated by the Russians.

Disaffection had begun to spread through the regiment's ranks. In the end, the unit – or what was left of it – had been labelled unreliable and sent to the western front, where the men had been used as a labour force on the so-called Atlantic Wall.

'We were afraid that when the invasion came, we would be sent to Germany – even back to Russia,' the man said. 'Either would have been a death sentence for us. We are no longer of any use to the Germans, and if we were to be taken by the Russians we would be shot out of hand for having served in the German Army. We knew from gossip and rumours that the invasion was coming soon, so we decided to desert. We split into small groups and hid in the woods. The plan was to join forces as soon as we heard the invasion had begun, then give ourselves up to the English or the Americans. They would not give us up to the Russians, would they?'

There was a pleading look in his eyes. He already knew that they were British Commandos, for Conolly had told him, and he was desperate for reassurance.

Receiving none, the man lowered his head again. 'The Germans have been searching these woods for us for days,' he said. 'Somehow, we have always managed to avoid them. If it came to it, we would have fought, for most of us are armed, but none of us wants to die. Not now.'

He stared up, his eyes wild. 'I wish to surrender to you,' he said to Conolly. 'Let me take you to where the rest are hiding. It is not far away, and the Germans have all left the area.'

Conolly translated for Douglas's benefit, emphasising the point that the deserters were armed.

'Could come in handy if we find ourselves in a tight spot,' he pointed out.

'These chaps are desperate to give themselves up, and they'll fight their way through the German lines if need be. What d'you reckon? Douglas's private army,' he grinned.

'Well, we'd better take a look at them,' Douglas grunted. 'You and I will go along. Stan,' he said to Brough, 'you stay here and keep an eye on things. We'll be back before long.'

He and Conolly inserted clips of ammunition into their MP-40s and stuffed some more into their pockets, then set off through the trees with the Ukrainian. The deserters, it appeared, had taken refuge in a railway tunnel, about a mile and a half away. The tunnel was disused, the line that led to it having been blasted by Allied air attacks during the preceding weeks.

Picking their way around old bomb craters that scarred the surrounding fields, they eventually came to the tunnel entrance. The Ukrainian went on ahead and called out something in his native language. There was a reply, followed by a brief exchange of words.

Men, all of them emaciated, some of them as ragged as scarecrows, began to emerge into the daylight. They formed up in a group, shuffling and uncertain, in front of the two SAS officers.

Douglas lowered his gun and looked at his companion, who had been counting the Ukrainians as they left the tunnel.

'Jesus,' Conolly said quietly.

There were two hundred of them.

CHAPTER ELEVEN

'Talk about feeding the five thousand,' Conolly muttered. 'That's knocked a hole in the rations, and no mistake.'

He was right. The enemy truck had contained just enough food and drink to cater for each man, and was now stripped bare. The Ukrainians were now sitting or lying among the trees, their stomachs full for the first time in days. Lambert had been going around issuing cigarettes to them. He came back wrinkling his nose.

'Smelly lot,' he said. 'Could probably do with a good delousing, too.'

'I don't suppose we're all that savoury ourselves,' Douglas reminded him. To luxuriate in a hot bath, he thought, would be a truly wondrous experience.

Conolly and Brough had checked the Ukrainians' weapons while the men ate and drank. They were armed mostly with Mauser 98K rifles, many of which were dirty, and each man had a few rounds of 7.9-mm ammunition. Some had steel helmets, others forage caps, but for the most part they were bare headed.

There seemed to be no one in overall command of the Ukrainians, so Douglas had decided to use the man Barber had captured – his name was Andrei Buchada – as an intermediary, with Conolly acting as interpreter. He summoned Andrei now, and told him exactly what was required.

'You must make it clear to your friends,' he said crisply,

'that I am in sole command of them and that they are my prisoners. I shall allow them to retain their weapons, because they will need them if we encounter any German troops. However, there are certain conditions which I must impose.'

Andrei nodded eagerly as Conolly translated, and Douglas was aware that he had assumed an awesome responsibility. Andrei and the other Ukrainians were depending on him utterly. They expected him to work miracles.

'The first condition,' Douglas said, 'is that your men must clean themselves up. Tell them to go off, one group at a time, and bathe in the stream that runs past the western side of the wood. Tell them, if possible, to shave also, and to wash their uniform. My plan depends on them passing for normal German soldiers. Do you understand?'

Andrei said that he did. Douglas nodded. 'Good. The second condition is that they must clean their weapons thoroughly. My officers and I will carry out a personal inspection to see that this has been done. There is plenty of time in which to carry out these tasks, because I do not intend to make any move away from here until after dark. Everything must be ready by then.'

As the day wore on, the morale of the Ukrainians underwent an astonishing transformation. Small groups detached themselves and went off through the wood to bathe in the stream Douglas had mentioned; so, at intervals, did all the members of Douglas's group, Colette finding herself a secluded spot where she could wash apart fom the rest. The SAS men's packs contained cakes of carbolic soap, which they handed over to the Ukrainians when they had finished with them themselves. Somehow, they managed to make each cake of soap eke out between nearly thirty men.

Throughout the day, the thunder of guns rolled across the *bocage* from the fighting on the coast. Swarms of Allied aircraft flew overhead, and Douglas noticed that they had black and white stripes painted under their wings. Sometimes, a section of aircraft would break away and swoop down to attack some unseen target in the distance.

Sometimes, too, sections of the horizon erupted in distant

fountains of black smoke when no aircraft were to be seen, as the mighty warships offshore hurled their fifteen-inch shells far inland. The Ukrainians watched in awe, some crossing themselves and muttering prayers of thanks that their God had seen fit to deliver them from the terror that was descending on the Normandy coast.

It was strange, Douglas thought, to be a distant bystander while history was being made. He had no idea what was happening on the beaches, but no doubt ever crossed his mind that the invasion would be successful.

He spent a long time that afternoon poring over his map, and discussing with Conolly and Brough the best way of reaching the coast. In the end they decided to head due west for twenty miles, wherever possible staying clear of roads and following the disrupted railway line that ran from Lisieux to Caen. In this way they hoped to swing behind the battlefront, then turn abruptly north to bluff or fight their way through the enemy lines and reach the coast somewhere near Ouistreham.

They set out as soon as it was dark, using the tunnel where the Ukrainians had sheltered as their starting point. They marched in single file, keeping to either side of the track, and as he marched Douglas thought that surely no British officer in history could have had a stranger command.

Progress was slow, for they often had to make detours around the bomb craters that pitted the ground. The sky was dark, with a fierce wind still driving clouds from the south-west, but in the early hours of the morning the stars came out, pale against the gun-flashes that flickered continually in the north and west.

Shortly before dawn, they made a three-mile detour across country to avoid the village of Mézidon, passing through more wooded country to pick up their railway line again at a spot where it ran parallel to the Lisieux-Caen road. Douglas dared follow the line no further, and so ordered his men to take refuge in a large apple orchard. They lay there in complete silence, shrouded in a dawn mist that clung close to the ground. Through Conolly, Douglas instructed the Ukrainians to maintain complete silence; somewhere not too far away he could hear the sound of engines, but it needed better light before he could assess the situation. He knew that they had so far travelled about half the planned distance.

As the mist began to disperse in the morning light, Douglas and Conolly crept to the western edge of the orchard and surveyed the land beyond. In the distance they could just make out Caen, with smoke rising from various points around it. In between was the ever-present *bocage*, with its high hedges and embankments that gave the little enclosed fields of Normandy shelter from the cruel Atlantic winds.

A river, which Douglas identified from his map as the Dives, twisted through the countryside, running from south to north and the sea. From that direction, as though its beginning had been signalled by the dawn, came renewed sounds of heavy fighting.

Beyond the river, the mist parted to reveal enemy tanks, positioned at intervals along the road that led to Caen. Douglas focused Conolly's binoculars on them, and saw that each tank was surrounded by a group of German soldiers. The tanks were all facing north, hidden behind the embankment that bordered the road. The soldiers were digging, piling earth in front of the armoured monsters. Other troops were draping camouflage netting over the Tigers, to conceal them from air reconnaissance.

Douglas counted twenty tanks; there were perhaps more hidden round a bend further up the road. Their field of fire covered the whole arc of ground to the west of the river, and Douglas realized that once the camouflage preparations were completed, the tanks would be invisible to anyone approaching from the north.

'I wonder why they're digging in?' Conolly said. 'They'd be more effective in a manoeuvring battle.'

'It's probably because they've run out of fuel,' Douglas told him, handing over the binoculars. 'Take a look at the divisional marking on the turret of the nearest one – I think it's the same unit that was laagered in the valley.'

Conolly studied the tank. 'So it is,' he said. 'They're obviously expecting some trouble, and you know what that means, don't you? The invasion has succeeded, and our boys are getting ready to advance inland. It's my bet they're planning to take Caen as the first major objective, then push out armoured spearheads to Rouen and Paris. If they can do that, they will create a big pocket, with most of the German forces trapped inside it.'

Douglas was looking at the road, and the ground to the south of it.

'I wonder,' he said thoughtfully, 'if there's anything we can do about those tanks? We've plenty of men, and if we work our way round into those fields over there we'll be hidden by the embankment on the south side of the road as we approach it. The Germans won't be expecting trouble from that quarter. We can take them by surprise. Split up our chaps into assault groups, say ten men to each tank. We might not get 'em all, but we'll get some. If we can knock off the Huns, we can maybe remove the breech mechanisms from the tanks' guns and dump them in the river.'

Conolly shook his head in mock sadness. 'Boss, I do wish you hadn't read so many *Boy's Own Paper* adventure stories when you were young.' He looked at Douglas. 'Are you *quite* determined to go ahead with this?'

Douglas grinned at him. 'Oh, absolutely,' he said.

Conolly sighed. 'I was afraid of that. Well, let's go back and give the others the good news.'

They went back to where the others were still lying under cover in the trees. On Conolly's instructions, Andrei picked out twenty Ukrainians who were to act as group leaders, although in seven cases they would be merely deputies, the groups being led by Douglas and the other SAS men. Colette protested about the fact that she was not to be permitted to lead a group, but Douglas was adamant. She would bring up the rear of his own group.

With the help of Conolly, Douglas gave the Ukrainians a thorough briefing. Each assault group would be assigned its own tank. The Tigers were spread out along a half-mile stretch of road, so the assault groups would remain in sight of one another, and would attack simultaneously. Douglas assigned Conolly, Brough, Lambert and Barber to lead the groups on the left flank; he, together with Olds and Mitchell, would lead the assault on the right, the three Ukrainian-led groups falling in between.

Some of the Ukrainians looked unhappy at being called upon to go into action, so Douglas asked Andrei to explain to them that the tanks must be neutralized in order to save many Allied lives, and they appeared to accept his orders without question. He hoped that they would prove reliable.

The briefing over, he drew Brough and Conolly to one side.

'Don't waste time on disabling the tanks if you run into serious trouble,' he told them quietly. 'We don't know what's round that bend in the road. If the odds are too big for you to handle, get out fast and fall back towards the river. We'll cover you.'

Splitting into their small groups, they made their exit from the apple orchard on its southern side, having first made sure that the coast was clear, trotting down into the fields and crossing the river by means of a small stone bridge, gradually moving round in an arc so that they were spread out in line with the road. Douglas knew that he was taking an enormous gamble, and the wait until all the assault groups were in position was long and agonizing.

At last, the signal came back along the line that all was ready. Douglas raised his arm, making a forward chopping motion, and led his group towards the tall hedgerow.

He reached the embankment and, lying flat, wriggled up its slope until he lay hard by the hedge. To his relief, he found that it was not thick and densely tangled like an English hedge, but was made of some kind of brushwood through which a passage could be forced without too much trouble. On the other side of the hedge he could hear the sound of picks and shovels at work, and laboured German voices.

His heart pounding, he looked back at his own group. One of the men signalled that he was ready, and Douglas took it to

135

mean that they all were. Colette, bringing up the rear, was armed with the Luger.

On Douglas's left, Brian Olds was looking at him expectantly from a position about forty yards away.

Douglas peeped through a narrow gap in the hedge. He could see some of the men who were working around the tank; most were bare to the waist, and he counted eight of them.

From his coat pocket, he took his last remaining grenade. Holding down the lever, he extracted the pin with his teeth. Then he let go of the lever, counted off two seconds and lobbed the missile over the hedge, ducking down behind the embankment as he did so.

The grenade went off with a sharp crack and metal fragments lashed through the top of the hedge. There was a scream, not so much of pain but of surprise and fear.

Douglas was already on his feet and bursting through the hedge, right shoulder first, the muzzle of his MP-40 pointing upwards to prevent its becoming snagged in the brush. He swung the barrel down as he landed on the other side, firing through the dust and smoke kicked up by the grenade and jumping across a body that lay in the road. By the time the others came through the hedge his sub-machine-gun had already done most of the work, cutting down several of the Germans where they stood. All along the road, the rattle of gunfire told him that the other groups were also engaging their targets.

Leaving the Ukrainians to finish off the other Germans, Douglas bounded on to the rear of the tank. The hatch stood open and the SAS officer poked the muzzle of his MP-40 through it, loosing off a burst and hearing his bullets clanging and zipping around the interior.

When he looked inside, he found that the interior was empty. Jumping through the hatch, he swung down past the commander's seat and looked around. The inside of the turret smelt of sweat and oil.

Douglas had once been a tank commander himself, and knew his way about. He had no difficulty in removing the breech block from the Tiger's main gun, and heaved it up through the open hatch to be received by one of the Ukrainians who ran across the field with it and hurled it into the river.

Douglas clambered from the tank and dropped to the ground. One by one the other groups were coming in, each one carrying a breech block which they dumped into the river in turn.

Down the road, the groups on the left flank were still firing. Douglas, using sign language, ordered the Ukrainians to spread out in a line with their backs to the river and lie down, ready to provide covering fire for the other groups if need be. The latter came back in short rushes, dropping every so often to fire at something unseen, and it was some minutes before Conolly, breathing hard, reached Douglas.

'German infantry, coming down the road,' he gasped. 'Lots of 'em. Time we got out of it. We lost a couple of Ukrainians.'

Douglas waved his arm towards the north. 'Fall back!' he yelled. 'Follow the river!'

They ran hard, heading for the next embankment, and went swarming over it, taking cover behind. Douglas looked back, just in time to see some enemy soldiers jumping through the hedge that concealed the tanks.

By this time, the Ukrainians had spread out behind the embankment and were shooting back. The Germans on the other side of the field wavered, and finding no cover vanished behind the hedge once more.

'Keep on falling back,' Douglas shouted, and Conolly repeated the command in German. The Ukrainians and the SAS group withdrew to the next embankment. When they reached it, Douglas turned to Conolly: 'Hold on a minute. We haven't much ammo left. We can't go on fighting these holding actions; the Huns will be all over us shortly. Listen to that shooting in the north; it sounds pretty close to me. Let's head in that direction as fast as we can. Come on, Colette – not far to go now!'

They set off again at a run, conserving their remaining ammunition and trying to ignore the shots that went crackling overhead from the guns of their pursuers. The firing was becoming more accurate, and Douglas saw two more of the Ukrainians go down.

Then Brian Olds, who was running along beside him, gave a sharp cry and fell sprawling.

With a sick feeling, Douglas swung round and went down on one knee beside his troop sergeant, who was clutching his thigh. Blood welled between his fingers.

'It's okay, sir,' Olds gasped. 'I think it went straight through. I can make it.'

With Douglas's help, he dragged himself to his feet and stumbled on to the next embankment, about fifty yards away. Conolly was a few yards ahead of them, shouting to the Ukrainians to keep spread out. They had a tendency to bunch together as they ran, presenting easier targets to the pursuing enemy.

Douglas pulled Olds through the hedge and they slid down the other side of the embankment, lying against the grassy slope to get their breath. The Ukrainians and some of the SAS men were lying on top of the embankment, firing across the field they had just crossed.

Mitchell slid down beside Douglas and unslung his radio. It had been shattered by bullets. He patted it affectionately then tossed it aside before scrambling back up the embankment. His MP-40 chattered as he loosed off short bursts in the direction of the enemy.

Meanwhile, Douglas cut away part of Olds' trouser leg. As the troop sergeant had suspected, the bullet had gone straight through. There was a neat, purple hole in the back of the thigh, and the bullet had travelled through the fleshy part to remove a sizeable chunk of flesh at its exit point.

Douglas found a field dressing in his pack and handed it to Colette, who began to bandage the wound expertly. 'You're lucky, Brian,' he said. 'I don't think there'll be any permanent damage. It looks worse than it is, but it will hurt.'

'Can't feel a thing at the moment,' Olds told him. 'It's just numb.' He looked down at the wound, and a sudden alarming thought struck him.

'Couple of inches to the right and higher up, and I'd be singing falsetto. Beg your pardon, miss,' he added in sudden embarrassment.

'That's all right, Brian,' Colette smiled. 'Just stop wriggling about.'

Douglas suddenly raised his head, cocking it to one side in a listening attitude. 'What's that?' he asked.

Colette and Olds had heard it too, above the rattle of the gunfire.

'Tanks,' Olds said grimly. 'And it's coming from somewhere over there.' He pointed towards the next embankment, the one on the northern side of the field where they had taken refuge.

The noise of tracks and powerful engines grew louder. Douglas looked around for some way of escape. There was none, short of plunging into the river.

'Just a minute,' Olds said, listening intently. 'Those don't sound like Maybach engines. They're more like –' He stopped, his eyes fixed on the far embankment. A large chunk of it suddenly trembled, heaved and then collapsed outwards into the field. A cloud of dust rose, mingled with clods of earth and fragmented scrub.

A tank stood in the gap. It was fitted with a device that looked like a bulldozer blade. Above it, the tank's gun wavered slowly from side to side, like a monstrous proboscis sniffing the air. The tank was an American Sherman.

Douglas and the others could just see the helmeted head of a man protruding from the turret. He was crouching behind a machine-gun. A moment later the weapon hammered, and a stream of bullets ripped into the ground just short of the hedgerow where the SAS men and the Ukrainians were lying.

Colette cried out. Before Douglas could stop her, she jumped to her feet and ran towards the armoured vehicle, frantically waving a square of white bandage above her head. The tank's machine-gun fired again and Colette swerved wildly, causing Douglas to think, for a terrible heart-stopping moment, that she had been hit.

Then the fire stopped, and the man in the turret swivelled the machine-gun until its barrel was pointing upwards. He rose a little higher, so that his shoulders and the upper half of his body were visible.

Colette reached the tank and spoke to him. She waved to Douglas, who helped Olds to his feet and draped the troop sergeant's arm around his shoulder. As he did so, two more tanks burst through the embankment and stood motionless, their engines idling. They, too, were fitted with bulldozer blades.

'Fall back!' Douglas shouted. 'Get behind the tanks!'

The Shermans reversed a little as the men streamed back towards the far embankment, the Ukrainians carrying their wounded with them. They poured through the gaps that had been punched by the tanks and gathered in the stone-walled field beyond. As soon as they were all safely through the Shermans moved forward again into the gaps. Their machine-guns opened up a heavy fire on the opposite embankment, compelling the German infantry to withdraw; then the commanders of the Shermans, not knowing whether the enemy had anti-tank weapons or not, reversed once more and remained hull-down behind the embankment.

The crews of the Shermans were British. Douglas jumped up on to the engine compartment of the tank that had appeared first and spoke to its commander.

'There's a third of a division of Tiger tanks a few fields away, over there,' he shouted. 'We've neutralized most of 'em by removing their breech blocks. If you whistle up some help fast you will be able to break through. The whole road to Caen is wide open.'

The young tank commander shook his head reluctantly. 'Against orders, I'm afraid. We were ordered to carry out a recce until we met opposition, then pull back. Not much I can do with six tanks, anyway, especially these. Bloody Shermans are useless against Tigers.'

'Damn!' Douglas swore. 'Look, can't you get on the radio and call up some reinforcements? If we give the Huns time to replace those breech blocks, they'll knock hell out of any advance that comes this way. Those Tigers are well dug in. What's more, they haven't got any fuel, so they aren't going anywhere.'

The tank commander stared at him. 'The woman said you were a British officer. Just who are you, exactly?' His eyes roved over Douglas's ragged French civilian clothing.

Douglas told him. 'Oh, well . . . that's different, sir,' said the tank commander, who was a second lieutenant. 'Just wait a moment, please.'

He vanished inside the Sherman's turret and Douglas heard him making a call over the radio. He re-emerged a couple of minutes later, looking uncomfortable.

'Sorry, it's out of the question. Brigade is quite adamant. We're to pull back. Our job is to guard a bridge across the Dives, about a mile and a half down river. A paratroop company captured it and held it for twenty-four hours before we got through to them. Brigade has promised to lay on some naval gunfire, though. There are some big battlewagons off the coast, and your Tigers are well within range of their shells. We'd better start moving.'

He looked at the Ukrainains, who were huddled wearily in small groups. 'God knows what we're going to do with this lot,' he said. 'The prison cages at the beach-heads are already overflowing. I see some of them are wounded; we can carry those on the tanks.'

Douglas jumped down from the Sherman and summoned Conolly. Together, they sought out Andrei, and found him on his knees, tending an injured man. He rose as they approached, handing over his task to someone else.

Through Conolly, Douglas said: 'Andrei, place your wounded on the tanks. How many are there?'

'Eleven,' the Ukrainian told him sadly, 'one seriously. And we suffered seven dead.'

'I'm sorry about that,' Douglas told him. 'It might have been a lot worse. Anyway, it's over for you now. Tell your men to leave their weapons here. They will have no further use for them, and after all you are prisoners.'

The sas officer smiled, and looked gravely at Andrei. 'I

don't think we could have made it without you,' he said, extending his hand. 'I hope all goes well for you.'

Andrei clasped Douglas's hand, then stepped back a pace. He straightened his grimy forage cap and saluted before turning away to issue orders to his men.

A few minutes later the six Shermans – three at the front and three at the rear of the column of marching men – were churning back across country, following their own track marks. There had been no further interference from the enemy, who had not put in an appearance since the Shermans opened fire on them.

After a while, Douglas and the others began to see tangible signs of the invasion; discarded parachutes in the fields, and then several gliders, all bearing the black and white invasion stripes, their tails removed to enable equipment to be taken out. One glider lay in a crumpled, splintered heap beside a row of trees through which it appeared to have crashed, and there were freshly dug mounds of earth in a row beside it.

At last they came to the bridge, where more Sherman tanks and some anti-tank guns were sited in defensive positions. British troops stared in surprise as the Ukrainians marched across, guarded by what appeared to be half a dozen villainous-looking French Resistance men and one woman.

There was a command post a little way to the rear, and in it Douglas found a harassed and very tired lieutenant-colonel of the Warwickshire Regiment, whose troops had relieved the original force of paras. He offered Douglas a large cognac and a cigarette, both of which the SAS officer accepted gratefully.

'You're in the front line, Douglas,' the infantry officer told him. 'This is as far as we've got. We're on the left flank of the advance from what we call Sword Beach. The other two British beaches, Gold and Juno, have joined up and have got to within about four miles of Caen and a couple of miles of Bayeux, but they are meeting with some pretty stiff resistance. Some enemy armour drove a wedge between us and them yesterday afternoon, too, but it's being mopped up.'

Overhead, there was a fearsome screeching noise. 'Ours,' the lieutenant-colonel said. 'Let's go outside and watch.'

142

Looking up, it was actually possible to see the dark shapes of the fifteen-inch naval shells. The air was filled with their crackling roar. They plunged down into the *bocage*, their great thudding explosions pounding the earth, pounding the spot where Douglas and his men had so recently been. The noise was deafening, denying speech and battering the eardrums.

The shelling went on for a full five minutes, then the terrible noise was cut off abruptly, leaving a leaden silence. In the distance columns of smoke rose into the morning air, their tops spreading out and joining up to form a great pall that drifted slowly on the wind. Wordlessly, the two men went back inside the command post.

'The Yanks have had a hard time of it,' the infantry officer, whose name was Bligh, told Douglas. 'They took a lot of casualties on one of their beaches, and their air drops ran into much tougher opposition than expected.' He ran a weary hand across his forehead.

'Anyway, we're ashore now. The beach-heads are secure and masses of material are pouring in all the time. Monty is planning a big offensive designed to take Caen in the next day or two, but he's being cautious. He's waiting until he has plenty of fresh troops, tanks and artillery. God knows, we're in no state to do much more.'

Bligh's eyes were haunted. The images of the previous day were still before him: the murderous fire on the beaches themselves, with bodies lapping the waterline and maimed men dying in minefields. Then the push inland, a few hundred yards at a time, the dusty, sweat-sodden men trudging in uneven lines on either side of the narrow roads while their supporting tanks roared past them. Shells bursting in the fields, bringing soil and pebbles and slivers of steel down on the men who sprawled on the earth; other shells bursting on the road itself, ripping men to pieces. Woods, echoing with the sudden clatter of machine-guns; little farmhouses, shattered and burning. The bodies of enemy snipers, with chickens pecking unconcernedly around them. An elderly couple, weeping beside their ruined home and shaking their fists at their liberators.

'There's still a long way to go,' Bligh said, 'before this is over.'

'Don't I know it,' Douglas agreed. 'By the way, I have a wounded man. Is there any chance of a lift down to the coast?'

'I'll arrange for a supply truck to take you down,' Bligh said. 'Report to the beachmaster when you get there, and he'll sort you out. One word of warning, though – don't go wandering off. There are mines all over the place. Make sure you follow the white tapes.'

'Thanks, and good luck.' Douglas shook Bligh's hand and went outside, joining the rest of the group while they waited for the promised truck. They sat by the road leading to the captured bridge and watched the Ukrainian prisoners being led away to whatever fate awaited them, escorted by military policemen.

As the column's head reached the SAS group, a command rang out. The marching Ukrainians' shoulders came back, and a hundred and eighty pairs of eyes turned in Douglas's direction. He stood up, feeling a little ridiculous in his French rags, and yet at the same time proud, to acknowledge the salute.

One of the MPs stared at him, then turned to address a companion. 'Bloody Frogs,' he said in a loud voice. 'Makes you wonder whose side they're on.'

He was doubtless surprised by a response from one of the group by the roadside. 'And you,' roared Stan Brough in a much louder voice, 'can piss off!'

CHAPTER TWELVE

The tide of war had flowed past Bayeux, leaving the ancient town unspoiled. Douglas stared in fascination at the shop windows as the jeep cruised past; they were empty of everything except piles of Camembert cheeses.

There were a few people in the streets. They took no notice of the jeep and its occupants, for the vehicle was only one of thousands that had passed through the cobbled streets since the Germans had pulled out in the second week of June.

That had been more than three weeks ago. It was now Friday, the seventh of July, a month since the invasion, and the Allies were preparing for the great assault on Caen, which still continued to hold out.

The jeep turned a corner. Conolly, who was driving, spotted an old, timbered building on the other side of the road. A sign above the door said *Restaurant de Touriste*.

'Are we classed as tourists, do you think?' Conolly asked, bringing the jeep to a stop outside.

'Don't know about that,' Douglas replied, 'but a glass of wine and some cheese wouldn't come amiss. We'll give it a try.'

They got out of the jeep. Both were wearing khaki battledress and red berets, and each wore the blue-and-white parachute insignia of the Special Air Service above his left breast. They were also armed with Sten guns, which they took into the building with them.

The entrance opened directly on to a large, cool room, with tables and chairs scattered haphazardly around it and a bar at the other end. The place was deserted. Conolly and Douglas approached the bar and the Irishman banged his fist on it several times. Presently, a door behind the bar opened and a thin-faced, elderly man with a drooping grey moustache shuffled through. He stood there, rubbing his hands on a dirty apron and gazing at the newcomers through watery eyes. The expression on his face was sullen.

Conolly ordered two glasses of wine and some cheese. Without a word, the old man placed two glasses on the bar top and produced a bottle of wine, which he placed next to them. He shuffled away to bring the cheese, and the two SAS officers wandered over to a table by the window. As they sat there, the occasional passer-by stared at them with an expression that was equally as sullen as the old bartender's.

'Cheerful-looking bastards, aren't they?' Conolly said. 'Anyone would think they didn't want to be liberated.'

'Maybe they didn't,' Douglas commented. 'It doesn't look as though they've had a particularly rough time.'

The old man brought their cheese, together with a few pieces of bread, and stared in disgust at the 'liberation' currency which Conolly handed to him in payment. He was by no means mollified by the Irishman's remark that the newly minted notes could be redeemed for real francs when the French monetary system was stabilized once more.

Conolly, visibly annoyed by the man's attitude, asked him point-blank what was the matter. The barman stared at him for a moment, then said with a shrug: 'Bah! We were all of us here behind *le Maréchal* and the National Revolution.'

He referred to Marshal Pétain, the hero of Verdun in the previous war and the French head of state since the armistice of 1940. 'We did not want a war,' he continued. 'We did not want de Gaulle and his dreams of a new France. We did not want millions of men and thousands of tanks to invade our beaches and our fields. Who knows what will happen now?'

Douglas and Conolly stood up, very slowly. 'Liam,' Douglas said quietly, 'you'd better tell him. My French isn't up to it.'

'Ah, what's the use?' Conolly snapped. 'It would be a waste of breath.' He picked up the wine bottle and headed for the door, followed by Douglas.

Outside, Conolly slammed the palm of his hand furiously down on the jeep's bonnet.

'Steady on, Liam,' Douglas warned. 'Don't get upset just because of that old sod.'

They got back into the jeep and lit cigarettes. Conolly inhaled deeply, then said: 'It isn't just the attitude of people like that. It's everything. Take London, for example.'

'I'd rather leave it,' Douglas grunted. 'But I think I know what you mean.'

On their earlier return from France they had gone to London for their de-briefing. Although they had failed in their planned mission to kill Rommel, they had good reason to be satisfied with their other achievements, which had contributed in no small measure to the successful breakout from the Normandy beach-heads. They had found, too, the answer to a question which had been in their minds; an aerial reconnaissance photograph, taken on the day after the invasion, had shown the bridge at Mantes, collapsed into the Seine in three places. A large number of tanks stood nose to tail on the road to the north of the river.

Olivier, it seemed, had carried out his task admirably.

Douglas and the others had found London depressing. There had been no particular reason, none that any of them could have described, unless it was that England's capital was once again under siege, the target of the German V-1 flying bombs. Londoners had withstood the *Blitz* of 1940 and 1941 with their characteristic courage and humour, but this was something different – something utterly impersonal and sinister. Whether London could go on 'taking it' was a matter open to serious doubt.

Colette had gone off to the headquarters of the Special Operations Executive for her own de-briefing, after which she had travelled to Scotland. The plan had been for Douglas to join her there, but it had not worked out. Instead, he and Conolly had been ordered to join the staff of Montgomery's

21st Army Group as Special Forces' liaison officers, and had spent a month in London, attending numerous briefings and delivering lectures – mainly to US Rangers – before being packed off to Normandy once more. The rest of Douglas's SAS detachment had been dispersed among various training establishments, much to their disgust – all except for Olds, who had departed for his home in Norfolk with a heavy bandage around his thigh and a broad smile on his face.

Douglas and Conolly, having completed their series of briefings, were now on their way to rejoin Montgomery's HQ, which was located in an apple orchard somewhere to the south of Bayeux. Both were still feeling rather bilious from the effects of the Channel crossing, which had been made on a fast and very bouncy naval launch.

They finished their cigarettes and drove on, passing through the outskirts of the town, and after getting lost several times eventually found the HQ, which was carefully concealed and camouflaged. They reported directly to Montgomery, who, dressed in his customary khaki slacks, grey pullover and black beret, was poring over a large map with several of his staff officers.

He looked up as the two SAS officers entered his command post. They saluted him and he returned their salute, as punctilious as ever.

'Wait outside for a moment,' he said crisply. 'I will join you.'

Montgomery emerged in due course, and invited them to join him in a stroll through the orchard. The morning was fine. Somewhere in the distance, artillery rumbled. The commander of the 21st Army Group launched into what he had to say without preamble.

'The assault on Caen begins tonight,' he told them. 'It will be preceded by a very heavy bombing attack, followed by an artillery bombardment. It is hoped that this concentration of firepower will destroy the enemy's will to resist.'

Montgomery looked at Douglas and Conolly in turn, then said: 'You will remember Major Fitzroy.' Both men nodded.

'I have received reports from French agents that he is still alive,' Montgomery said. 'It appears that he was taken to Bayeux for interrogation, then removed to a German military hospital in Caen. I want you to go into Caen with the infantry assault, locate him and bring him out. The Germans must not be allowed to evacuate him. Major Fitzroy has certain knowledge that would be very valuable to them, knowledge of matters which have far greater military significance even than the recent invasion. With hindsight, he should never have been sent to France in the first place, but that is another matter.'

He paused, then went on: 'The assault goes in at dawn tomorrow. Use whatever methods you think best to carry out this mission. You have a completely free hand. I have signed the necessary authority for you both. That is all. Good luck.'

He handed them each a piece of paper, then turned and strode back to his command post. They looked at what he had given them, and Conolly let out a low whistle. The document, instructing all ranks of the British and US Armies to give all possible assistance to the SAS officers, was not merely signed by Montgomery; it also bore the signature of General Dwight D. Eisenhower, the Supreme Allied Commander.

'This is powerful stuff,' Conolly said. 'We could go a long way on this. I didn't know Major Fitzroy was such a VIP. Wonder what he's been up to?'

'It's not our business to wonder, Liam,' Douglas said firmly. 'It's good to know that Fitzroy made it, though, even if he is a prisoner. Come on – we've got a lot of planning to do.'

It was late afternoon when Douglas and Conolly arrived at the front line and reported to the headquarters of an armoured brigade which was to take part in the initial assault. The brigadier inspected their written authority with considerable surprise.

'Well,' he said, 'I'll be happy to have you tag along with us, and of course I'll give you all the help I can. Your objective is quite close to our line of attack, in fact. I assume you've studied a map of the city?'

Douglas said that they had. 'But I've a feeling it might not be of much use after the air force has done with the place,' he commented. 'We might need one of your tanks to force a way through the rubble. I know its a lot to ask, but this mission is extremely important.'

'Obviously,' the brigadier said, glancing again at the signatures in front of him. He handed the papers back to the SAS officers. 'Douglas,' he said musingly. 'Weren't you once a tank man yourself?'

'That's right, sir,' Douglas told him. 'Twentieth Hussars, in the desert.'

'Thought I'd come across the name somewhere,' the brigadier said. 'Those were the days. None of this bloody *bocage* to contend with then.'

They reminisced for a while, then Douglas and Conolly went off to get some food, the brigadier giving them a warning to be on the lookout for snipers.

'Lots of them about. We practically live in our tanks because of them. One of our chaps got out to relieve himself in a shell-hole this very morning and got shot in the arse. Luckily, the bullet only went through the fleshy part. But don't go wandering off, whatever you do.'

Later, after they had eaten, Douglas and Conolly surveyed the ground that lay between the tanks' position and Caen through a periscope. It was a nightmare vista of death and destruction, for terrible battles had been fought over this ten square miles of Normandy during the past fortnight. The ground was torn, scarred and slashed by shellfire and tank tracks; Panther and Tiger tanks lay drunkenly across ditches where the anti-tank guns had caught them, their plates already rusting from the effects of the sharp summer showers.

Clouds of flies buzzed around their open turrets, a grim reminder that the remains of the crews were still inside. An overpowering stench of death and decay, aggravated by the hot sun, lay over everything.

The British tank men called this terrible wasteland Epsom Downs.

The evening drew on, and by ten o'clock dusk was falling. Douglas and Conolly had been dozing when the thunder of massed aero-engines roused them. They looked to the north, into a cloudless, electric blue sky.

As far as they could see, a stream of bombers stretched back towards England. The aircraft were still above the earth's shadow, the evening sun shining golden on the metal of their wings and fuselages. Ahead of the main stream came the pathfinders, passing over the heads of the watching troops. The leading files turned away to the right, back towards the coast. Flares showered down over Caen in a golden rain, dropping in spiralling cascades towards the doomed city.

Flak began to blossom around the main bomber stream until the sky was covered with black puffs. The bombers flew on, seemingly unconcerned, although in reality they must have been buffeted by the thousands of explosions and torn by millions of splinters. Only one dropped away, falling slowly into the shadows, livid flames flaring from its ruptured fuel tanks. It vanished beyond the town.

The deep thud of explosions merged into a single, continuous thunderclap of sound. Smoke rose slowly into the sky over Caen, rising to meet the last of the marker flares as they drifted down. Rank after rank of the bombers dropped their loads and wheeled away, racing the approaching night as they headed back to their English bases.

The onslaught lasted forty-five minutes. In that time, little more than the blink of an eye when viewed in the context of a war that had already dragged on for almost five years, nearly a thousand heavy bombers unloaded three thousand tons of bombs and smashed Caen to rubble from end to end.

And still it was not over. After the bombers had gone, and darkness shot by the flames of the burning city fell over the land, field artillery and the guns of warships continued to pound the ruins, so that the ancient buildings of the city where the remains of the Conqueror had once lain were destroyed several times over.

With the dawn, the British and Canadian divisions moved into the attack. They met with stiff resistance. The men of the 12th ss Panzer Division, most of them barely eighteen-years old, crawled out of holes in the ground, salvaged whatever tanks and guns they could, and fought a fanatical defensive battle, destroying over a hundred British tanks in the course of the day.

Mindful of their task. Douglas and Conolly were little more than observers as the battle unfolded. The British tanks were powerless to penetrate the rubble-blocked streets; walls were still standing, but the closely packed stone houses had been flattened. The battle for Caen became a battle of machine-gun and mortar, of vicious engagements between opposing platoon and section commanders. As the British and Canadians advanced, yard by yard, fire from snipers who still lay concealed among the rubble caused more casualties among them, and mines also took their toll.

Even as the fighting continued, French civilians emerged dazed from their cellars and stood amid the drifting clouds of smoke and dust, staring in shocked horror and disbelief at what the thousands of tons of bombs and eighty thousand shells had done to their city. Then, with gunfire crackling around their ears, they began to claw at the ruins in search of their dead and injured.

The end of the day found the two SAS officers, sweat-stained and begrimed from the smoke and stone dust, crouching behind a pile of fallen masonry near what had once been the University of Caen. Machine-guns and mortars were in action among the ruins, the Canadian soldiers crouching behind piles of books in the University library.

Douglas dragged a plan of the town from a pocket of his battledress blouse and examined it.

'The German hospital was supposed to be somewhere about here,' he said, his voice hoarse with dust. 'It ought to be over on our right, but I'm damned if I can make head or tail of anything. Let's take a look; keep your head down.'

They scrambled over more ruined stonework and dashed across a rubble-choked street, throwing themselves under cover on the opposite side. The heads of two Canadian soldiers popped up from a nearby shell-hole.

One of them looked at Douglas's red beret in surprise. 'Airborne,' he said. 'Didn't know any of you guys were involved in this.'

'Special job,' Douglas told him. 'We're looking for the German military hospital.'

'You're lying in it,' the Canadian said, 'or what's left of it. It got flattened last night. Fritz got most of the guys out, though; they're in the Abbaye aux Hommes, back there.' He jerked a thumb over his shoulder.

Douglas looked. Some distance away a great cathedral stood, its spires ravaged by shellfire, with smoke drifting around it. Its massive walls seemed to have withstood the worst of the bombardment.

'Thanks,' Douglas said. 'Come on, Liam.'

They dodged away among the ruins, dropping flat in the dust every now and then as an enemy mortar bomb exploded nearby. Presently, they reached a high wall, surmounted by railings, which enclosed the abbey and its spacious grounds. The grounds were now a maze of craters, and splintered trees lay haphazardly across them.

As they approached the great porch, a strange and unnerving sound came to them above the roar of the fighting that racked the city. It was a murmuring, but more than that; mingling with it was a low wailing, a sobbing undertone.

They stepped into the church. The evening sunlight beamed down through gaps in the roof, falling on a tormented scene.

The great stone floor, strewn with straw, was littered with people; aged, middle-aged and young, crowded together like sardines in misery. The limbs of many were wrapped in bloody rags. Most were civilians, a few of the survivors of the holocaust that had overwhelmed Caen, and from these the tortured murmurings arose.

My God, thought Douglas, aghast. We have done this to them . . .

'Over there,' Conolly said roughly, masking his emotions. He pointed to a corner of the church, where British and German medical orderlies were moving among rows of stretchers.

Douglas looked for an officer, and eventually found a Royal Army Medical Corps captain administering morphine to a German soldier who had lost both legs below the knee. He waited until the doctor had finished his task, then went up to him and asked if he could spare a moment.

'No, I can't,' the captain said brusquely. 'Look around you, and you'll see why. What is it you want?'

'I'm looking for a British officer,' Douglas told him. 'A Major Fitzroy. The Germans had him in their military hospital. We have orders to find him.'

He showed the captain his authority. The RAMC officer was not impressed.

'There were a few British in the German hospital,' he said. 'Some of them have already gone back to the rear, but there are a few on those stretchers over there, by the wall. They are all in a pretty bad way. Take a look, by all means; the name Fitzroy doesn't ring a bell, though.'

Followed by Conolly, Douglas stepped carefully over rows of wounded men and came to the place indicated by the captain, where some twenty stretchers were laid in a row.

They passed along the line of pain, peering at each taut, drawn face. Half way along the line, they stopped by a man whose emaciated features were partly concealed by a growth of beard. He stared up at them with opaque, watery eyes.

Heedless of the dirt on the floor, Douglas knelt beside the stretcher. There was a lump in his throat. 'Hello, Walter,' he said gently.

Fitzroy's eyelids moved. 'Who is it?' he asked, in a voice so faint that Douglas could barely hear it.

'It's Douglas. Callum Douglas. Conolly is here, too. We've come to get you out of this.'

Fitzroy shook his head from side to side. 'Too late, old boy. I've had it. They had to take the old arm off . . . gangrene, you know. Good to see you, though.'

The voice was a little stronger. Douglas stood up and turned to Conolly. 'Go and see the doc. Find out if we can move him.'

Conolly nodded and went back through the rows of

154

wounded in search of the RAMC captain. Douglas knelt again, and said: 'We'll have you out of here, don't worry. You'll be as right as rain in no time. Anyway, we have orders to bring you out. Monty's orders. Can't go against those, can we?'

Fitzroy reached up suddenly, his right hand seizing Douglas's sleeve in a surprisingly strong grip. 'Callum,' he said urgently, 'come here. Right down, so that nobody else can hear.'

Douglas bent right down so that his ear was close to Fitzroy's mouth. The grip on Douglas's sleeve tightened.

'Listen carefully, and don't interrupt. There isn't much time.' The weak eyes held Douglas in an unblinking gaze.

'Very soon – perhaps in only two weeks' time – there is going to be an attempt on Hitler's life. The likelihood is that it will succeed. The Nazis will be overthrown and replaced by a new military regime, with Rommel at its head. Don't ask me how I know! It happens to be true.'

Fitzroy swallowed drily, and Douglas gave him a drink from his water bottle. Fitzroy thanked him, then continued: 'Rommel apparently does not know that his name is on the conspirators' list, but they are confident that he will go along with their plans once Hitler has been killed. After that there will be a negotiated peace. Representatives on both sides are waiting to bring an end to . . . all this.'

Fitzroy was breathing hard now, as though the effort of speaking had drained his last reserve of strength. When he spoke, his voice was faint once more. 'Callum . . . go back and tell Monty that the German representative is ready to make contact as soon as Hitler dies. Tell him it is . . .'

'Yes? Go on, Walter. Who?'

The words were no more than a whisper, a rustle of grass. 'Rommel's second in command. General Speidel.'

Slowly, Douglas stood up. Conolly was at his elbow. The Irishman shook his head. 'He can't be moved,' he said. 'He's too weak.'

Douglas stood in silence for a moment, looking down at the figure on the stretcher.

'It doesn't matter, Liam. He's gone. One of the bravest men I have ever known.'

The words, even as he spoke them, sounded trite, unworthy of the man Fitzroy had really been.

Together, the two SAS officers drew themselves up and saluted. Then they turned away and passed from the place of pain, out into the shattered city.

EPILOGUE

October 14th, 1944

The Opel staff car stood by the side of the road, its engine switched off. A man sat in the back seat, gazing up at the branches of the pine trees that flanked the road. It was a clear autumn morning, and the sun was warm.

A little farther along the road, two more men stood waiting. One was the driver of the car, the other a general. They seemed impatient, though anxious not to show it. Despite his anxiety, his natural fear of the unknown, the man who sat in the car permitted himself a smile. He could afford to keep them waiting a few seconds longer.

Nothing had been the same since that morning in July when a Spitfire had come streaking along the road in Normandy, without warning. Erwin Rommel himself had been seriously injured in the attack; he had been more fortunate than his driver, the faithful Corporal Daniel, who had died of his wounds several hours later.

The attack had come two days before the attempt on Hitler's life. It had been several weeks before Rommel had learned about that, as he lay in hospital, recovering from his wounds.

How ironic it was that he, who had survived shot and shell and attempts on his own life, should now be asked to die by his own hand! Asked, moreover, by Hitler himself, the *Führer* to whom Rommel had always remained loyal, even though he had sometimes questioned the leader's decisions and, in private, referred to him with contempt!

There had been terrible times since the abortive assassination attempt in July. Five thousand people had been put to death. Some were conspirators, others people who had merely known the conspirators, others still who had known nothing at all. They had died horribly, strung up on piano wire or meat hooks.

And now he, Rommel, was to die; and yet he had known nothing of the attempt, nothing of the fact that his name had been placed on some list by men with whom he had had no dealings.

He wished, now, that he had died in Normandy, under the cannon of the Spitfire. That, at least, would have been a death with honour.

He looked down at the little phial of poison that lay on the seat beside him. They had told him that it would work in three seconds. Best to get it over with now, before his thoughts turned to the wasted years, to the years in the service of a Reich which soon would no longer exist.

Lucie!

He raised the phial to his lips and drained it. There was a numbness in his mouth, then a brief moment of excruciating pain, and then a drifting.

And then they were all around him, the laughing, sunburned faces of his men. And the desert wind blew hot in the boiling dust, and there came the tang of diesel and the roar of engines as the Panzers churned over the road to Alamein.